NIGERIA
DEMOCRACY
WITHOUT
DEVELOPMENT
HOW TO FIX IT

OMANO EDIGHEJI

A'lime Media Limited
www.alime.media

ZEEZI OASIS
Leadership Inspiration

Bulk order information:
Special discounts are available on bulk purchases by government bodies,
corporations, associations, and others. For details, please contact the
publisher.

Cover Design Concept by Eikon Grae

First Published, 2020

ISBN
978-978-980-080-3

Designed and Published by: Zeezi Oasis Leadership
A'Lime Media Limited   Inspiration Ltd
7, Anjorin Lane, Off Adegoke Street,   Suites 27 - 28,
Surulere, Lagos, Nigeria.   2nd Floor, Tolse Plaza
                                              4 Franca Afegbua Crescent
+234 901 0000 120   Apo, Abuja
contact@alime.media   Nigeria
www.alime.media   zeezioasis2@gmail.com

NIGERIA
DEMOCRACY
WITHOUT
DEVELOPMENT
HOW TO FIX IT

OMANO EDIGHEJI

Praise for *Democracy Without Development*

"This book makes a worthy argument for a democracy of purpose. It is a timely call for democracy to propel institutions and measures that substantially improve the lives of citizens, develop the economy and improve the processes for selecting and electing leaders."

Mallam Nasir Ahmad El-Rufai,
Governor, Kaduna State, Nigeria.

"This is an authoritative book that is both theoretically and empirically grounded. It explains the paradox of democracy and development in Nigeria. Dr Edigheji proposes that for Nigeria to develop, its politics has to be driven by a developmentalist elite whose politics is anchored on the people and political parties based on ideology. He argues for a democratic developmental state for Nigeria to progress and prosper. This book is essential reading for anyone interested in understanding Nigeria's democracy and its poor development outcomes in the last 20 years."

Dr Kayode Fayemi,
Governor, Ekiti State, Nigeria.

"If you are interested in democratic development (in general), and concerned about Nigeria's fate (in particular), then *Democracy without Development* is just the book for you! Edigheji describes a series of developmental deficits in the country that he loves, and argues that these deficits must be overcome. By encouraging its elites to change their ideological orientation, and by pointing to the need to develop the state's structural capabilities, Edigheji shows us how Nigeria can—and should—become a democratic developmental state."

Professor Jonathon Moses,
Department of Sociology and Political Science,
Norwegian University of Science and Technology,
Trondheim, Norway.

"I commend Dr Omano Edigheji's book for its passionate plea to Nigerians to ensure democracy does not fail. The pathway he draws is that of a developmental state that replaces rent-seeking by a predatory class with structural transformation of the economy that produces dividends of democracy for the people."

Professor Jibrin Ibrahim,
Senior Fellow,
Centre for Democracy and Development.

"Dr Omano Edigheji's book adds in great measure to our ongoing quest as a scholarly community to understand why, despite the heavy investments made in promoting democratisation in Africa and the sacrifices that citizens have accepted as a price to pay for the success of democratic transitions, democracy has failed significantly to deliver development either by way of improvement in citizens' wellbeing and welfare or in terms of a sustained and inclusive pattern of economic growth that is usually accompanied by progressive social policies. Instead, despite episodes of growth fuelled by on-and-off commodity booms, the democratic experience is marked – and marred – by widespread poverty and deepening inequalities that threaten the long term sustainability of the entire political system if left unchecked. Dr

Edigheji, using Nigeria as a case study, underscores the point that democratisation without development amounts to an exercise in futility. His argument in favour of a democratic developmental order as an alternative is a compelling one worthy of rigorous consideration in policy and academic circles."

Professor Adebayo Olukoshi,
Director for Africa & West Asia, International IDEA.

"In Nigeria's *Democracy Without Development,* Omano Edigheji provides powerful insights and evidence for Nigeria's harvest of paradoxes. The failure of the political class to locate a moral compass has led to Nigeria's drift into rough seas of crippling poverty, grave leadership dysfunction and anomie in which violence of one form or another seem ever so close by. Omano's analytics is a worthy read for all but especially for the student of Development Studies and for policymakers."

Professor Pat Utomi,
Founder, Centre for Values in Leadership,
Lagos, Nigeria.

"In this book, Dr Edigheji examines the reasons for the retreat of democracy in Nigeria. He provides arguments that account for the failure of democracy to take firm root in the country. Dr Edigheji deserves our commendation for adding to the increasing literature on Nigeria's struggles to institutionalise democracy. This work should help outsiders appreciate the Nigerian condition, while it should hopefully offer new perspectives for further research."

Bishop Matthew Hassan Kukah,
Catholic Diocese of Sokoto, Nigeria.

"This is a bold and original work that extends research and ideas from political economy to the Nigerian democratic challenge. It is well-argued with insights, data and good literature review."

Dr Sam Amadi,
Former Chairman,
Nigerian Electricity Regulatory Commission.

"This is a seminal piece of work. Well-written, data-driven, theory-embedded and analytically-grounded."

Dr Ayokunu Adedokun,
Assistant Professor of Politics & International Development,
Leiden University, Netherlands.

"Dr Edigheji knows the story of Nigeria's democratic journey better than most people, primarily because the journey mirrors his: he was in the trenches during the quest for democracy and has continued to contribute to the country's evolution as a democracy. His book, *Nigeria: Democracy Without Development, How To Fit It*, is a practical rendition of what must be done to make democracy work for Nigeria and its people. It is historic as it offers prospects for the future. This is a very important book for anyone interested in understanding Nigeria and its quest for a just and equitable democratic country."

J.J. Omojuwa,
Author, *Digital: The New Code of Wealth*.

Praise for Democracy Without Development

Dedication

For my wife, Wendy and my boys, Zipho and Zinwe for their love, inspiration and sacrifices. You all are the sunshine in my life.

Contents

Chapter Three
Nigerian Political Leadership: The Lack of
Ideology of Development Nationalism and
Valueless Politics

Chapter Four
The Institutional Deficits of Nigerian
Democracy

Tables

List of Figures

Preface

Across the globe, the relationship between democracy and development has preoccupied policy makers and scholars alike. There is a general assumption that democracy leads to inclusive sustainable social and economic development. Whether this is the reality is debatable, given the fact that the world has witnessed undemocratic regimes that have achieved remarkable social and economic development. In the same vein, some democratic governments have recorded poor development outcomes. Though the relationship between democracy and development is tenuous, authoritarian development is unsustainable in the long run. In addition, besides its substantive outcomes, democracy is worth pursuing and celebrating in its own right. Whilst the rule of law, political and civil liberties are key characteristics of democracy and necessary, they are not sufficient conditions for the enhancement of human dignity, and consequently for a country to be classified as a democracy. The quest for democracy by citizens is premised on the expectation that democracy will enhance their living standards. This aspiration is mostly being dashed across the world, especially in Africa.

In Nigeria, the struggle for democracy, led by the pro-democracy movement, was not only to give repressive military regimes the boot, but also in the hope that it would reduce poverty, inequality and unemployment, provide public goods to citizens and transform the structure of the economy. Nigerians particularly market women, artisans, students, workers and others from different walks of life, the true heroes of democracy - had hoped that democracy would lead to inclusive social and economic development as well as better management of the economy. Basically, they expected that democracy would result in better management of the country's resources.

However, in the two decades of democracy, 1999 – 2019, there has been a paradoxical relationship between democracy and development. During the period under review, Nigeria's experience has been marked by increased poverty, inequality, unemployment, underemployment, insecurity, ethno-religious divisions, increased corruption and, continued dependence on oil as the major source of government revenue and foreign exchange. The aspiration that by 2020, Nigeria would be one of the 20 leading economies in the world has not been met. Also unattained are the Millennium Development Goals (MDGs) and with these bleak antecedents, it is unlikely that the Sustainable Development Goals (SDGs) and the African continent's development goal, African Agenda 2063, will be achieved with the current political trajectory.

Nigerian developmental failures are primarily due to inadequate investment by the Nigerian political class in human capital development in education, health, skills and competencies that will enable individuals live a dignified and a happy life. Because of inadequate investment in its people, Nigeria is unable to take advantage of the youth bulge to spur its development. In this book, I will demonstrate that the political class has largely limited the roles of the youth in the political process to the disreputable parts such as being the political thugs responsible for unleashing mayhem before, during and after elections.

This book demonstrates that majority of Nigerians have been excluded from the benefits of democracy. The life of the average Nigerian is that of misery and squalor, which gives rise to frustration among the citizenry. Instead of freedom, democracy has given rise to illiberty. The lack of development dividends has consequently eroded the credibility and legitimacy of democracy in the country.

This book explains the factors that account for the rising poverty, inequality, unemployment, and the general deteriorating conditions of Nigerians, while the economy benefits the wealthy few, especially politicians who have used the state as a means to private accumulation rather than the provision of basic services to the people. It is ironic that the main beneficiaries of democracy in Nigeria, the political class (some of whom were apologists of military rule) are the same people that undermine democracy in the country. This elite have institutionalised corruption as a national norm. In this book, I argue that the absence of a developmentalist elite to dominate the political arena politics without principles; and the capture of the state through a non-merit based recruitment of both political leaders and civil servants account for democracy without development in Nigeria. Simply put, two factors account for democracy without development in Nigeria: poor political leadership and weak institutions. With amoral politics and the worship of the *Nigerian god*, political leaders have created a society without a moral compass. This partly accounts for the high level of insecurity in the country.

Nigeria Democracy Without Development proffers solutions to save the Nigerian democracy, ensure that it delivers development dividends to Nigerians, and promotes the industrialisation and high value added service sector so that ultimately Nigeria becomes a country of producers rather than consumers. Consequently, I call for Nigeria to build a Democratic Developmental State (DDS). To be clear, Nigerians need a state that is both developmental and democratic. These two must go hand-in-hand. This becomes more imperative given that military regimes that hijacked governance did not develop the country, therefore Nigeria can ill-afford a repressive regime ever again. Authoritarian regimes are certainly not the answers to Nigeria's development challenges. Comparative experiences, such as that of South Korea, have shown that authoritarian developmental states are unsustainable in the long run. Democratic developmentalism remains the most sustainable form of governance. However, to have positive development impact on Nigerians, democracy must go beyond the ritual of elections every four years.

This book is unlike most scholarly and policy works that focus on electoralism. These works focused on the wrong institutions that do not lead to development. These scholars and international development agencies like the World Bank usually focused on good governance. Like some institutionists, I argue that there is no correlation between the good governance indicators and development, hence the contention in this book that Nigeria needs to build inclusive and transformative institutions to develop. Also, there must be an end to the phenomenon of godfatherism that manipulates the political process for personal gains and desecrates the electoral process. Using the analytical lens of developmentalism, I shall demonstrate that Nigeria is not a democracy.

There are three critical components of DDS that Nigeria must focus on to achieve democratic development. The first component is that a political elite with an ideology of development nationalism that will prioritise investment in Nigeria's greatest asset - its people - must become the most dominant actors in politics. The enhancement of human well-being must be the primary goal of the DDS. Secondly, such an elite must transform the structure of the economy by promoting industrialisation – manufacturing, agro-allied industry and high value added services. In other words, it must create a viable post-oil economy. Importantly, it should promote the digital economy and combat the challenges of climate change. Lastly, the achievement of the above will be dependent on the elite building inclusive political and economic institutions (the latter would require creating the enabling environment for women and youths to participate in the economy and the political process). This will include building and enhancing the political, organisational and technical capacities of the state.

The technical capacity would require a merit-based bureaucracy and the non-politicisation of the civil service. I argue that Nigeria's development would be dependent on strong economic and political institutions championed by a developmentalist-oriented elite. As shown in this book, this will require ideologically-driven political parties anchored on the aspirations of the people.

xxvii

Nigeria: Democracy without Development. How to fix it

Chapter One

Background to Democracy in Nigeria

Introduction

On May 29, 1999, Nigeria returned to democratic rule and embraced democracy as its preferred form of government. The country had two previous experiments with democratic rule. The first lasted from independence in 1960 to October 1966, when the first military coup put an end to the First Republic. The Second Republic lasted only four years and three months before it met the same fate. The military handed over to the elected government under President Alhaji Shehu Shagari on October 1, 1979, but the military once again took over power in a coup on January 1, 1984 with General Muhammadu Buhari as Head of State.

This book examines the critical factors why successive administrations in the democratic period have failed to create equitable development and social and economic justice for a majority of its people. Specifically, it explores why an electoral democracy, with its representative system of government, has in the last two decades been incapable of meeting the needs of its citizens and responding to their aspirations for improved living conditions. There has therefore been a paradoxical relationship between liberal democracy and development in the country.

Furthermore, this book analyses the root causes of Nigeria's democratic failures through an institutional analysis by focusing on both structural and agent-based (human agency) factors of the state. In other words, why the leadership (both political and administrative) and the quality of the bureaucracy of the Nigerian state have not been able to promote inclusive development and social justice. This is what one of the world's leading scholars of state capacity, Linda Weiss (2010) referred to as the "hardware" and the "software" of the state. The hardware of the state is the administrative and organisational structures as well as technical attributes, which constitute the internal institutional structures of the state that shape development outcomes, while the "software" of the state is the "ideological orientation" of the political class, which sets the context for the "normative-political environment that supports and sustains the political will to pursue developmental projects" (Weiss, 2010: 9).

Identifiable weaknesses in these two key components mean the Nigerian state lacks the internal organisational architecture and ideological orientation to promote inclusive sustainable development. While the democratic era has experienced remarkable economic growth, it has not been beneficial to a

Nigeria: Democracy without Development. How to fix it

2

majority of its people. Due to social and economic exclusions, and an absence of the "dividends of democracy", Nigerians are questioning the quality of constitutional democracy. This gap between expectations and results — development outcomes — will be the focus of this book. Indeed, one of the main points of this book is that the foundation of Nigerian democracy is flawed. This is because it is built on a state that is neither democratic or developmental. Consequently, it is not able to promote inclusive sustainable social and economic development. As a result, I argue for the establishment of a Democratic Developmental State in Nigeria that will ensure the sustainability of constitutional democracy, lead to a structural transformation of the economy by moving both labour and capital from low to high productivity sectors, and to enhance the wellbeing of Nigerians.

In light of the above, this book focuses on the ideological orientation and the political, organisational, administrative and technical capacities of the Nigerian state that have resulted in developmental deficits in the democratic dispensation which in turn is eroding the people's confidence in the democratic system. By contrast, most existing studies on democracy in Nigeria and elsewhere have focused on the rule of law, transparency, accountability, civil and political rights. These are necessary, but are not sufficient conditions to achieve equitable development, gender and ethnic justice, and youth empowerment. I argue that it is the ideological orientation and the structural capabilities (institutional architecture) of the state that lead to economic transformation, as well as result in inclusive economic outcomes and social justice. By structural capabilities, I mean the administrative, technical, organisational and political capacities of the state.

Two factors are crucial for the developmental success of a country, namely leadership and institutions. These are discussed in detail in this book. A democratic developmental state will ensure social and economic inclusion. It will also reduce inequality and enhance human wellbeing. These are necessary conditions for the sustainability of any electoral democracy. I also argue that electoral democracy in the country is fragile because it is catering to the interests of the political class and a few economic elites, while failing to invest in the country's greatest assets: its people—most of whom are poor, uneducated, unemployed or underemployed. This has given rise to growing insecurity in the country. As a result, the frontiers of freedom, instead of expanding, are shrinking.

This book uses an institutional analysis framework to discuss democracy in Nigeria and its outcomes. This is not to be institutionally deterministic but to show that the development deficits of the democratic period is largely attributable to the country's weak and flawed institutional foundation and the ideological poverty of the political elite. Specifically, it draws on the democratic developmental state as a development theory, which argues for a merit-based and career-orientated public service with the strong political capacity in the context of democracy to drive a developmentalist agenda in the country. To achieve this will require ideological or programmes-driven political parties that are anchored on the wishes of the people.

The Nigerian Democratic Journey

Nigeria has experienced uninterrupted electoral democracy since May 29, 1999, after 16 years (1983-1999) of military dictatorships. This is the longest period of civilian rule in the post-independence period. The country has embraced a multi-party democracy with four elected presidents who have governed in succession. For the first time in its history, in May 2015, an incumbent president, Goodluck Jonathan of the People's Democratic Party (PDP) lost an election and conceded defeat to a former military leader from the opposition party, Muhammadu Buhari of the All Progressives Congress (APC). Buhari subsequently won re-election in February 2019 for a second term. Constitutional democracy has come to stay in Nigeria, even if this is only in theory, and despite the several challenges it faces. The era of military dictatorship seems to be well and truly over.

At this juncture, it is important to understand the factors and forces that gave rise to democracy in Nigeria like elsewhere on the African continent. The quest for democratisation was championed by citizens due to their lived realities of repression and impoverishment under military dictatorship and the need for improved livelihood. The latter was imperative given the social and economic crisis of the 1980s and 1990s, including scarcity of food items and the resultant inflation, which impoverished Nigerians. The macroeconomic instability resulted in the devaluation of the naira, and the country witnessed a process of de-industrialisation—the latter partly due to scarcity of foreign exchange to import raw materials needed by the manufacturing sector. Nigeria was on its knees and in spite of this, when Nigerians were asked in 1985 if they would accept a loan from the International Monetary Fund (IMF) with its attendant conditionalities, majority of them said "no". But the "poll" was a ruse. General Ibrahim Babangida merely used the non-poll to push the narrative that he was a military ruler that listened to people.

This was the context in which Babangida introduced what he termed "home grown Structural Adjustment Programme" (SAP). It had all the major characteristics of the World Bank and International Monetary Fund (IMF) imposed austerity measures that Nigerians thought they had rejected—economic liberalisation, privatisation and commercialisation of State Owned Enterprises (SOEs), and the deregulation and reduction of the role of the state in the development process, including the provision of basic public goods. SAP negatively impacted the living standard of the Nigerian people.

Babangida also promised to return the country to civilian rule but it soon became clear that he was trying to extend his stay in power. It was in this context that the then president of the Nigerian Bar Association, Alao Aka-Bashorun, accused Babangida of having a "hidden agenda". Babangida's attempt to prolong his stay in power made Nigerians more determined to fight for freedom. Democratisation became the clarion call of the people. They were led by human rights groups, especially the Civil Liberties Organisation (CLO) under the leadership of Mr Olisa Agbakoba as president; the Committee for the Defence of Human Rights (CDHR) under Dr Beko Ransome-Kuti as president; and pro-democracy groups, especially the Campaign for Democracy (CD)[1] and Democratic Alternative (DA); students under the auspices of the National Association of Nigerian Students (NANS); progressive academics under the auspices of the Academic Staff Union of Universities (ASUU) and Women in Nigeria (WIN). They were supported by the progressive press and the Concerned Professionals.

---

[1] *The CD was formed in 1989 with President of the Nigerian Bar Association (NBA) Chief Alao Aka-Bashorun as its interim president. He was succeeded by Dr Beko-Ransome-Kuti as president. At the inaugural meeting in Jos, Chima Ubani was elected as Secretary General.*

To underscore the fact that the pro-democracy movement was also about improved livelihood and sustainable development, Nigerian students led the campaign against SAP in 1989, which began at the University of Benin, and the protest against the removal of petroleum subsidies in 1988, which started at the University of Jos. As Adebayo Olukoshi poignantly argued:

> ... the struggle for human rights and civil liberties, as well as democracy, became part and parcel of the struggle against social and political injustice in the context whose defining feature was authoritarian. Indeed, for some left activists, the vigorous campaign for human rights and civil liberties became one of the potent forms of struggle against the authoritarian, militarised state, *and for inclusive development* (Olukoshi, 1997: 163, *emphasis added*).

In all, contrary to Igbokwe (1999) who tried to make the struggle for democracy an elite project, the true heroes and heroines of the pro-democracy struggles were ordinary Nigerians, especially market women, workers, artisans and students. Within the pro-democracy movement, former student leaders including Chima Ubani, Femi Falana, Emma Ezeazu, Chom Bagu, Innocent Chukwuma, Omano Edigheji, Salihu Lukman, Ogaga Ifowodo, Bamidele Aturu, Olaitan Oyerinde, Sylvester Odion-Akhaine and Uche Onyeagucha argued within the CD that there should be mass mobilisation against the annulment of the June 12, 1993 presidential elections. The street mobilisations spearheaded by the CD forced General Ibrahim Babangida to "step aside" and hand over power in 1993, to a military-civilian contraption called the Interim National Government (ING) headed by Ernest Shonekan.

It is important not to sectionalise the struggle for democracy. The narrative in some quarters that the June 12 struggle, cum, the struggle for democracy, was championed by a section of the country - the South West - is incorrect, and that narrative tends to diminish the importance of the quest by the Nigerian people for democracy. The CD that led the struggle for democracy was a pan-Nigerian organisation. Its activists were drawn from all parts of the country. Its Chief Strategist, Chima Ubani, who served as Secretary General, was not from the South West geopolitical zone. Also, the trade unions, especially the National Union of Petroleum and Gas Workers (NUPENG) and the Petroleum and Natural Gas Senior Staff Association (PENGASSAN) that joined the struggle and played important roles were pan-Nigerian bodies. In 1994, these two unions embarked on the longest strike in the history of Nigeria and almost brought the country to its knees as part of the democratic struggle.

In the course of the struggle, a number of pro-democracy leaders such as Dr Beko Ransome-Kuti, Chief Gani Fawehinmi, Femi Falana, Chima Ubani, Ken Saro-Wiwa, Baba Omojola, Ogaga Ifowodo, Abdul Oroh, Bamidele Aturu, Omano Edigheji and Innocent Chukwuma were detained. The winner of the 1993 presidential elections, Chief M.K.O. Abiola, was also detained and died in prison in 1998 under mysterious circumstances.

A number of journalists such as Nosa Igiebor and Onome Osifo-Whiskey (*Tell* Magazine) and Babafemi Ojudu and Dapo Olorunyomi (*The News* Magazine) were detained. Others such as Bagauda Kaltho (*The News* Magazine) and Tunde Oladepo (*The Guardian*) were killed. The publisher of *The Guardian*, Alex Ibru, was shot by agents of the military regime but escaped with injuries.

Several activists were not as lucky as they were killed by the military regimes of General Ibrahim Babangida and General Sani Abacha. Among these were Alhaja Kudirat Abiola (wife of M.K.O. Abiola), Alhaja Suliat Adedeji and Chief Alfred Rewane (a major financier of National Democratic Coalition (NADECO). Though not exhaustive, this long list of people maimed or killed (including hundreds of ordinary Nigerians) demonstrate the severity of the repression by the military regime targeted at those who fought for democracy.

To be clear, politicians, including those under the auspices of the NADECO played a supportive role in the struggle for democracy. However, their role was limited to press releases and mobilising the international community. As a former president of the National Association of Nigerian Students (NANS) and one of the key leaders of the struggle for democracy, Abdul Mahmud (2013) correctly noted:

> Claims have been made by Colonel Nyiam that the June 12 struggles were prosecuted by the National Democratic Coalition. Nothing could be further from the truth. Whilst it is important to stress that the National Democratic Coalition responded to the annulment of the June 12, 1993 presidential election in a propagandist way, typical of politicians, the Campaign for Democracy actively took the battles to the junta on our streets. Propaganda was useful only to the extent that it riled the junta. But, when the junta later descended on a section of the press that was sympathetic to June 12, propaganda became less of a tool for effective oppositional mobilisation.

For its activities, prominent members of NADECO were detained, some were killed or gravely wounded, and some went into exile. Suffice it to say that some of its leading members subsequently betrayed and abandoned the democratic struggle for the de-annulment of the June 12 presidential election, which has become synonymous with the struggle for democracy. Some became cabinet ministers under the General Abacha military regime; others became apologists for the regime.

This unprincipled nature of the political class has been carried over to the era of electoral democracy that I will discuss in subsequent chapters. The politicians who supported the pro-democracy movement had a narrow agenda, and a narrow understanding of democracy. To them democracy is a transition of power from the military to the civilian, with the politicians in charge of federal and state purses (Jega, 2001). This is unlike the radical activists, most of whom were members of the CD and DA who, to paraphrase Adebayo Olukoshi, had a broader understanding of democracy. This informed their agenda of the democratic struggle. In the words of Olukoshi, the radical activists:

> ...emphasise, in their articulation of the ... democratic project, political as well as economic and social elements. Democracy for them is not just a question of multiparty politics and electioneering even if the rights of the people to freely elect their leaders is recognised as non-negotiable; it includes a vast array of social and economic reforms whose adoption are widely perceived as being necessary for the establishment of a more just social order. It is a definition of democracy which necessarily calls for an interventionist, "developmentalist" state, not for the unbridled retrenchment of the state. It calls for the thorough reforming of the state and its broad-ranging restructuring in order to tackle the problem of state failure, but it also firmly rejects the World Bank/IMF program for the re-definition of the role of the state. For these groups, there is a fundamental incompatibility between structural adjustment

and democratisation… (Olukoshi, 1998: 45).

It is important to note that progressive academics produced scholarly works to promote the democratic project. Democratisation was not an externally driven project. Olukoshi, one of Africa's leading development scholars also aptly observed:

> The attempt towards resurgence in democratic forms of participation was borne out of the frustration that accumulated over a period of the last two decades of political crisis and instability. It also flowed from mass disillusionment following the period of economic crisis and social decay that we witnessed in the 1980s as structural adjustment programmes began to bite across the continent (Olukoshi, 2011: 11).

Similarly, Laakso and Olukoshi (1996: 25-26) note that the demands of Nigerians and scholars in their democratic struggles "was for a political reform programme that would extend and guarantee economic and social democracy to the masses with the aim of empowering them and enabling them to redress their exclusion from decision-making processes that affect their lives".

The struggle for democracy was not just to do away with military dictatorship; it was also a struggle for qualitative improvement of their living conditions. Therefore, the quest for democracy cannot be separated from the quest by citizens for improved livelihoods and enhanced human wellbeing. Nigerians expected that democracy would deliver development and reduce poverty. It was also a struggle to preserve the earth. It is in context of the latter that it is important to understand the involvement of environmental groups such as the Movement for the Survival of Ogoni People (MOSOP) and the Environmental Rights Action (ERA) in the democratic struggle.

Since the onset of democracy, Nigeria has made progress in civil and political liberties. The press is relatively freer now when compared to the 1980s, and with the emergence of social media in the last few years, Nigerians are using platforms such as Twitter, Facebook, WhatsApp, Instagram and blogging to speak up and hold the government accountable. With millions of mobile phones in the hands of Nigerians, ordinary people have turned into citizen-journalists. With hashtags on Twitter, citizens readily spread information about bad governance across the globe. One good example is the #BringBackOurGirls hashtag about the kidnapped Chibok schoolgirls in Nigeria by Boko Haram. While former President Goodluck Jonathan was denying the kidnapping of the girls, ordinary Nigerians, through the hashtag, campaigned to alert the world about the plight of the kidnapped Chiboks girls. Soon, celebrities including then American first lady, Michelle Obama, joined the #BringBackOurGirls campaign. Other popular hashtags include #OccupyNigeria, which was to protest against the Federal Government's removal of fuel subsidy. Social media is therefore contributing to the promotion of free speech and the deepening of democracy in the country. However, the use of social media has some shortcomings such as the spread of fake news. Regardless, there has been marked progress in the area of civil and political liberties.

Democracy in Nigeria, like the rest of the African continent, has been marked by increasing cases of electoral violence "which is geared towards winning political competition of power through violence, subverting the ends of the electoral and political process" (Atuobi, 2008). Election-related violence takes various forms, namely intimidation of opponents, killings (about 150 people were killed in the period leading up to, and during the 2019 General Elections.[2] Yet, this was considered to be one of the most peaceful elections in the twenty year period of electoralism); kidnappings; destruction of property (both private and political party/actors' properties); thuggery and disruptions of rallies and meetings; arbitrary detentions; arrest of opponents and so on.

Social divisions—ethnic, religious and others—have been the root causes of election violence in the country, as well as the winner-takes-all attitude prevalent in Nigerian politics. In addition, with state power being a means to accumulate wealth, elections have become "do-or-die" affairs in the country as politicians take steps to subvert the electoral process and the will of the people. Weak and compromised law enforcement agencies and the judiciary have equally created fertile grounds for electoral violence, with the perpetrators knowing that they are unlikely to be sanctioned for their crimes against the state and the Nigerian people.

Political leaders have exhibited the attributes of both toxic and transactional leadership, focusing on their personal interests with little regard for long-term national interests. In addition, the political elite have acted with impunity and have devised several ways to subvert electoral democracy. The attempt by former President Olusegun Obasanjo to seek a constitutional amendment to secure a third term is a good example of how politicians of the Fourth Republic have attempted to undermine electoral democracy.

---

[2] *See Report of the European Observation Mission to the Nigerian 2019 elections.*

Former President Barack Obama at the 16th Nelson Mandela Annual Lecture on July 17, 2018 in Johannesburg, South Africa, eloquently captured the dangers that those in power and their business associates pose to democracy on the continent, including Nigeria. It is ironic that its main beneficiaries, the political class, are the people undermining liberal democracy. According to him, the trend is "whereby elections and some pretence of democracy are maintained – the form of it – but those in power seek to undermine every institution or norm that gives democracy a meaning" (Obama, 2018).

Subversion of the electoral process and the principles of good governance by politicians pose a great danger to democracy in Nigeria. As former Head of State, General Abdulsalami Abubakar correctly observed, the resort by politicians to "electoral fraud poses a major challenge to democracy in Nigeria and by implication, poses a threat to the security of the nation. Electoral fraud desecrates the sanctity of democracy and weakens its capacity as an instrument for the mobilisation of human and material resources for the development of the people and the state" (cited in Okeshola, 2011: 151). In general, the electoral process is fraught with irregularities.

All of the above are threats to constitutional democracy in the country. The self-centredness of the political class constitutes a major factor for the ruination of Nigeria and the condemnation of her people to lives of misery and squalor. Thus, the subversion of the rules of the game, deliberate undermining of the principles and institutions of good development governance, ideological poverty and naked corruption by the political class are some of the greatest dangers to the survival of democracy in the country. Others are weak and dysfunctional institutions, high level of insecurity and the fact that the majority of Nigerians have not benefitted, economically and socially from democracy. Holding regular elections is not enough to qualify Nigeria as being democratic.

Having set the context of democracy in the country, in the next chapter, I will proceed to discuss the ideological orientation that underpins it.

Book Outline

This introductory chapter is followed by Chapter Two which discusses the development outcomes of Nigerian democracy since 1999. The analysis in the chapter shows that electoral democracy has not resulted in the qualitative improvement of the living conditions of most Nigerians. Only the wealthy few and their hangers-on have benefitted. Also, there has been no significant structural transformation of the economy, which continues to be dependent on the production of crude oil, subsistence agriculture and other informal sector activities. The latter two are the main absorbers of labour in the country.

In Chapter Three, I cover the ideological orientation of the Nigerian political class. I argue that it is important to understand the institutional architecture of the state and the consequent development outcomes, that is, its impact on growth and development. Chapter Four focuses on the ideological and institutional underpinnings of democracy in the country. Specifically, it describes a political elite that lacks an ideology of development nationalism and the technical, administrative and organisational structures (institutions) of democracy. It shows that the managers of the Nigerian state, have neither the political nor technical capacity necessary to propel a structural transformation of the economy. They have also failed to formulate and implement any policy that could promote inclusive development, social justice and address the problem of climate change. The lack of political capacity is exemplified by the domination of the political landscape in the twenty years of democracy by political parties that lack any ideology.

Chapter Five, the concluding chapter, argues for a democratic developmental state, which is driven by a developmentalist elite that will establish political and economic institutions to achieve the developmental objectives of inclusive social and economic progress for all Nigerians. In fact, to overcome the current development deficits of democracy, Nigeria needs a political class that is principled and organised in clearly identifiable, ideologically-driven political parties, that will prioritise investment in human capital and infrastructure, thus promoting a structural transformation of the economy.

Chapter Two

The Development Deficits of Nigerian Democracy

Democracy, simply put, means development.
So that a country in which people go hungry is
not a democracy.

– *Professor Christopher Ryan Maboloc*

No Developmentalism, No Democracy

It is important that democracy is analysed through the lens of developmentalism. For our purposes, developmentalism means the structural transformation of an economy through industrialisation and the enhancement of human capabilities: human capital and ultimately human wellbeing. As Brian Keeley (2016) of the OECD rightly argues:

> Economic success crucially relies on Human Capital – the knowledge, skills, competencies and attributes that allow

people to contribute to their personal and social well-being, as well as that of their countries. Raising human capital does not only refer to education and training, but also to the improvement of health levels, community involvement and employment prospects. Focusing on the consistent development and upgrading of human capital at a national level should be a priority.

In fact, the expansion of human capabilities is the means and ultimate goal of development. The United Nations Economic Commission for Africa (ECA) defines structural transformation:

...as the change in the composition of GDP, such that the manufacturing and service sectors have progressively larger contributions than agriculture to growth. Structural transformation also implies a shift in the use of factors of production, such as labour, which is moved from low productivity (agriculture) to high productivity sectors (industry, including agro-industry) (ECA, 2016: 2).

Therefore, we will analyse the developmentalist project of democracy in Nigeria through its ability to enhance the productive capacities of the society, which involves structural transformation of the economy. This will require changes in the sectoral composition of industrial and economic output and employment, imports and exports and the ratio of imports to exports. It will also require the expansion of human capabilities which enhance the productivity, income and the assets of citizens. To draw on Amartya Sen (1990), political freedom enables citizens enjoy social and economic freedoms that should constitute the central analytical lens to assess democracy, because both development and democracy are mutually reinforcing. In this sense, "development includes a process of economic change involving the construction of a more complex and productive economy capable of generating material standard of living" (White, 1998: 20). This in turn legitimises democracy, as a number of scholars have correctly argued (Evans,

2010; Edigheji, 2005 and 2010; Olukoshi, 2011; Matlosa *et al.*, 2008).

The analysis in this book does not suggest that democracy impedes development. A simple statistical test that uses key indicators of political and civil liberties will show that there is no relationship between democracy and development. Also, democracy needs to be pursued for its normative values because, among others, civil and political rights are essential to upholding and enhancing human dignity. However, anecdotal evidence shows that a democracy that is unable to deliver inclusive development is not sustainable in the long run. In fact, for its sustainability and normative value, democracy is an agenda worth pursuing in its own right. Using the challenges faced by the authoritarian developmental state of South Korea, Eum Mee Kim (2010), made a strong and powerful argument for developmental democracy. This is because ultimately, "human progress is measured by the achievement of social justice and the elimination of poverty and oppression, not by unbridled accumulation of private wealth or naked exercise of power" (Gills, 2000: 10).

On the flip side, the inability of liberal democracy to create a shared future poses a great threat to national security. Democracy must focus on nation-building and development— meaning it must prioritise human security with the involvement of an active and informed citizenry. This paradigm of human security implies that conflicts arise from the inability of a socio-political system to satisfy the needs of its people. There is therefore a need for a paradigm shift in the conception of development and governance, that is, a shift from a narrow focus on macro-economic stability, military security and electoral democracy to a broad focus on social and economic justice, and participatory/cooperative governance.

In the absence of social and economic justice, there is no equality in liberal democracy. Democracy requires that all citizens have equal access to the basic essentials of human needs. White (1998) points to the danger of that deficit for democracy as follows:

> ...democratic citizenship is undermined if there is too great a contradiction between the egalitarian norms of a democratic polity and the inequalities of individuals and groups in civil society. Glaring inequalities undermine democracy in two basic ways; first, by fuelling social discontent and political instability and, second, through the persistence of poverty, by excluding more or less extensive sections of the population from access to the political process and its fruits (White, 1998: 28).

As he correctly argued, the social objectives that must be key elements of democratic developmentalism include:

> ...alleviation of absolute and relative poverty; the correction of glaring inequalities of social conditions (between genders, classes, regions, and ethnic groups); provision for personal safety and security; and the tackling of looming threats such as environmental degradation... Overall, to the extent that democratic polities are instrumental in organizing socio-economic progress along these lines, they can be described as developmentally successful; their success depends on the existence and efficacy of the democratic developmental state (White, 1998: 20).

Even in advanced democracies, when democratic dividends accrue disproportionately to the wealthy few and does not serve the interests of a majority of its citizens, their foundations have become shaky and some are unravelling. The rise of populism in the United States of America (USA) and Europe is partly due to the fact that democratic outcomes accrue to the wealthy few, while a majority of the people are unable to make ends meet.

Both Brexit and the presidency of Donald Trump have been linked to the rise of populism and divisive politics in Britain and the USA respectively. To a large degree, white supremacy groups (and other right-wing groups) have been emboldened in both countries. One consequence of this is that institutions and values that were sacrosanct in the US and Britain are no longer guaranteed with the rise of populism. Exclusionary democratic outcomes therefore threaten the foundations of liberal democracy.

While liberal democracy has normative values worth pursuing and celebrating in its own right, its perceived social and economic dividends are the major drivers why citizens desire and struggle for democracy. In the long run, the sustainability of democracy is dependent on its ability to deliver real social and economic benefits to a majority of the people. This is because "Citizens are able to exercise real choice and participate meaningfully and equally *in democracy* only after they have gone beyond poverty, squalor and inequality" (Mhone and Edigheji, 2003: 351, *emphasis added*). Poverty makes democracy fragile and lose credibility. Substantive democracy is therefore a *sine qua non* for the survival of formal democracy.

A democracy that is not able to deliver socio-economic benefits will end up in social and political instability. As Maboloc (2018: 2) correctly observed, "Democracy, simply put, means development. So that a country in which people go hungry is not a democracy." In fact, a democracy that is unable to enhance the wellbeing of its people stands on a weak foundation, and its legitimacy will eventually erode. As the Director of Political Affairs of the African Union, Kabele Matlosa (2019) succinctly puts it:

> Whatever model of democracy we conceive for Africa, it must be a democracy that addresses the basic needs and fundamental rights of Africans first and foremost ... democracy must put bread on the table for Africans...this is simply because people do not eat democracy. People eat food...Africa does not need democracy for democracy's sake. Africa therefore needs democracy for food and democracy for development's sake.

As I have argued elsewhere:

> ...the quest and struggles of the African people for democratic
> governance is not only to do away with repressive and
> autocratic governments but also that democracy would
> address their socio-economic conditions in a way that will lead
> to qualitative improvement in their material conditions. This
> has important political value. Citizens are able to exercise real
> choice after they have gone beyond poverty, squalor or
> ignorance as the latter problems constitute constraints on
> freedom and equality (Edigheji, 2005: 9).

Democracy must enable people engage in productive economic
activities in order to create wealth. This will require that democracy
create the conditions for citizens not only to increase their incomes but
their asset base. This is a necessary condition to create a shared and
sustainable future. However in Nigeria, politicians in the Fourth
Republic seem to underestimate the danger that a lack of development
dividends poses to democracy. Even before the advent of the Fourth
Republic, the late foremost Nigerian political scientist, Eme Awa
(1991) warned that a democracy that cannot deliver on the basic needs
of the people will be short-lived. In light of this, Igbuzor and Edigheji
(2003) argued that democracy and development must go hand-in-
hand. In fact, to take the conception of Nobel Laureate in Economics,
Amartya Sen (1990) "development as freedom", democracy is a
constituent part of development. Taken to its logical conclusion, a
liberal democracy that does not lead to qualitative improvement in the
lives of a majority of people is not developmental.

When democracy is unable to deliver social and economic benefits to
its citizens, there will be socio-political upheavals. For instance, there
is a causal link between poverty and terrorism in Africa. A World Bank
survey in 2011 showed that about 40% of those who join rebel
movements were motivated by a lack of jobs (see Annan, 2016).
Anecdotal evidence also points to a strong link between poverty and
terrorism, especially in developing countries. In addition, some
scholars such as Usman (2015) point to high levels of poverty and high
unemployment among the youths as contributing factors that make

them easy targets for recruitment by the Boko Haram terrorist organisation. While this is not a scientific study, Ayo Obe, one of the leaders of #BringBackOurGirls movement in a tweet on January 27, 2018 quoted Wale Edun as saying that in interviews conducted with twenty-six youths in the North East of Nigeria, twenty-five of them indicated that they wanted to join Boko Haram because they had no jobs, and only one indicated religion as a reason to join the terrorist organisation. Therefore, there is a causal link between the inability of democratic governments to deliver developmental dividends to a majority of their people and the rise of terrorism on the continent.

Development Outcomes of Nigerian Democracy

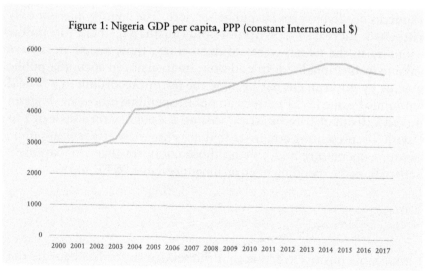

Figure 1: Nigeria GDP per capita, PPP (constant International $)

(Figure 1 Chart here. Source: World Bank, 2018a.)

The truth is that the economic growth in Nigeria in the twenty years of democracy has been impressive, but it has neither been sufficient or inclusive. Figure 1 shows that the standard of living of Nigerians has, on average, improved in the democratic period, with GDP per capita increasing from $2,848 in the year 2000 to $5,339 in 2017. But much of this increase, as well as the economic growth, has been beneficial to and enriched a narrow elite. The country has remained a low middle-income country in the Fourth Republic, with GNI per capita increasing from $270 dollars in 2000 to $2,450 in 2016 (World Bank, 2018a). This points to a lack of structural transformation in the economy, because most people continue to be engaged in low productivity agricultural and informal sector jobs. Successive administrations since 1999 have not invested much on infrastructure, health or education, which would have fostered an inclusive economy. It is no coincidence that Boko Haram originated in one of the poorest and most deprived areas of the country.

Nigeria has become more unequal and unfair. Not only does wealth not trickle down, but it is barely taxed, thereby depriving the state of resources needed to provide public services. The country has not only witnessed increased corruption and mismanagement of public resources in the twenty years of democracy, these social vices have become institutionalised. In addition, inefficiency in spending public revenue by government has become the norm. According to a World Economic Forum (WEF) survey on public spending efficiency, Nigeria ranked 120 out of 136 countries, scoring 2.2 out of 7 on a scale of 1 to 7, with 7 representing countries that are extremely efficient in public revenue expenditure and 1 being those countries that are extremely inefficient in the spending of government revenue (WEF, n.d).

Exclusionary Social Outcomes of Nigerian Democracy

A noticeable positive trend is that the service sector has become the main contributor to GDP, pointing to the gradual diversification of the Nigerian economy. Its contribution to GDP increased from 40.88% in the year 2000 to 56.93% in 2017. This is followed by agriculture, whose contribution to GDP increased from 19.23% in 2000 to 25.08% in 2017. In the same period, industry contribution to GDP declined from 29.02% in 2000 to 8.81% in 2017, while

Nigeria: Democracy without Development. How to fix it

24

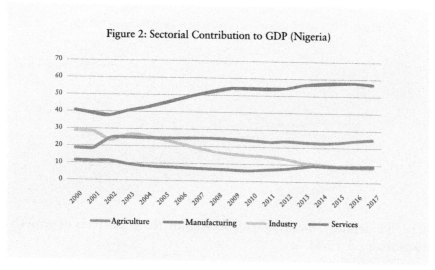

Figure 2: Sectorial Contribution to GDP (Nigeria)

Source: NBS Data, 2018.

manufacturing's contribution to GDP declined from 11.84% in 2000 to 9.18% in 2017 (NBS, 2018). John Page of the Brookings Institute draws attention to the nature of the shift of African economies, including Nigeria's when he observed that:

> Unlike the structural transformation seen in other regions, the shift away from agriculture hasn't been toward manufacturing and industry, but rather services. This shift is controversial: Many experts see this newer trend at odds with the successful development models in Asia as well as potentially hurting Africa by skipping over opportunities such as technology innovation, and policy experimentation and learning (Page, 2015: 32).

It is therefore important to understand the nature of the service sector in Nigeria. The two sub-sectors of services, namely ICT and financial services, are meant to be high value-added activities; however, their impact remained minimal (see Figure 3)even though their continued contribution to GDP has increased from 3.50% in 2000 to 11.67% in

25

Nigeria: Democracy without Development. How to fix it

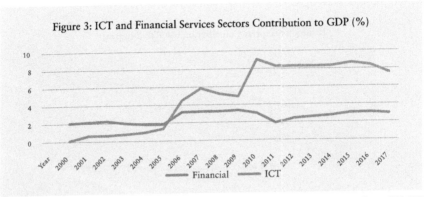

Figure 3: ICT and Financial Services Sectors Contribution to GDP (%)

Source: NBS, 2018

2017. Incidentally, these two sub-sectors are the key drivers of growth in a globalised world.

The point is that diversification in the economy, with the service sector as the largest contributor to GDP, is not creating jobs and it is not making a dent on poverty alleviation. Furthermore, the service sector is not making significant contributions to foreign exchange earnings or driving the competitiveness of the economy. This is because the activities in the sector are low value-added services. Also, the manufacturing contribution to GDP is now lower than what it was in the 1970s thus, Nigeria has remained a nation of consumers. This highlights the danger that if the country fails to develop its manufacturing and industrial sectors, as well as high productivity services, it will continue to be dependent on finished goods from the developed world. This will be a continued drain on its foreign exchange, which will make it even more vulnerable to the volatility of global commodity markets owing to the lack of structural transformation of the economy.

President Muhammadu Buhari underlined the importance of manufacturing to Nigeria's progress and prosperity in his address when he received the report of the Committee to Assess the Impact and Readiness of Nigeria on the Africa Continental Free Trade Agreement

Nigeria: Democracy without Development. How to fix it

26

(AFCFTA). According to President Buhari, "We have to develop policies that promote ... production" (Buhari, 2019a: 1) and to shift from the importation of goods. He correctly observed that "... many of the challenges we face today, whether security, economic or corruption are rooted in our inability, over the years, to domesticate the production of the most basic requirements and create jobs for our vibrant, young and dynamic population" (Buhari, 2019a: 2).

It is important to note that even if the decline in these sectors – manufacturing and agriculture – is a global trend, with the rise of the service sectors, it is imperative for Nigeria to aggressively pursue strategies that will grow its declining industry and manufacturing sectors, especially the latter because of its positive multiplier effects. In order for the country to develop, it needs a strong manufacturing and industrial base, which should be complemented by the promotion of agro-allied industries. This would be a sure way to generate sustainable high wage employment and sustainable growth: to change Nigeria from a country of consumers to producers and to create a shared future and inclusive development.

The economic growth that the country has experienced in the twenty-first century is not due to a fundamental structural transformation of the economy; rather, it is due to a rise in global oil prices. The structural nature of the economy and the dependence on the oil and gas sector makes it vulnerable to the volatilities of global oil prices. The consequences of the decline in global oil prices to sub-$30 per barrel in 2016, meant the Nigerian economy suffered a recession. The economy began to slow down in 2014 partly because of declining oil prices and the mismanagement of the economy under President Goodluck Jonathan's administration. The economy began to recover in 2017 with a growth rate of .83% and experienced a higher growth rate of 1.9% in 2018, because global oil prices maintained an average of $69.78 per barrel throughout the year.

27

Nigeria: Democracy without Development. How to fix it

Figure 4 shows the Nigerian GDP growth rate from the year 2000 to 2017.

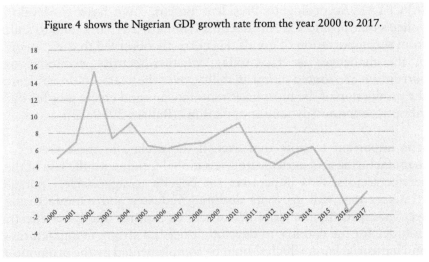

Source: NBS 2018

On average, the economy grew by 6.11% in the 18-year period between 1999 and 2017, of the democratic dispensation. However, the growth rate in the two decades of democracy is too low and it is obvious Nigeria will not meet the target of being one of the 20 largest economies in the world by the year 2020 as envisioned by its Vision 20:2020.

Also, the growth has been driven by a global commodity boom that led to a rise in global oil prices. In 2015, the growth rate declined astronomically due to a fall in global oil prices and by 2016, the Nigerian economy was in recession with a negative growth rate of -1.58%. The recession was also due in part to the mismanagement of the economy by the administration of President Goodluck Ebele Jonathan who ran the economy into a ditch by its unwillingness to save and its readiness to squander revenues from oil.

The narrow production base of the Nigerian economy is illustrated by its dependence on natural resources, namely agriculture and oil and gas. To illustrate the country's dependence on mineral resources, the oil and gas sector accounted for about 10% of GDP. Yet petroleum exports revenue represented over 90% of total exports, earning the country $877 billion in revenue under the democratic dispensation (May 1999–December 2017). With plummeting oil revenues, President Muhammadu Buhari's administration initially refused to devalue the naira, but its value declined by more than 30% in the parallel market from ₦200 to $1 in October 2015 to ₦363 to $1 in May 2018, and by June 2019, the value of the naira was ₦360 to $1. Importers, including those that import spare parts for manufacturing, as well as ordinary consumers, felt the adverse effects of the devaluation of the naira in the parallel market.

Another important factor in assessing Nigeria's development is how it affects its people, the country's most precious asset. As noted earlier, human capability enhancement is both a means and goal of development, a fact that is recognised by development scholars and agencies. It therefore constitutes an important analytical lens to assess Nigeria's democracy.

Unemployment and Underemployment in the Democratic Era

Due to the enclave nature of the Nigerian economy, majority of Nigerians eke out a living in an informal economy that is characterised by vulnerabilities that include lack of access to adequate financing, unstable employment and income and a near absence of basic social security and protection[3]. The enclave nature of the commodity sector is such that it is also unable to create employment for a majority of the people. There have been consistent increases in the number of unemployed people in the country, which rose from 3.3 million in 2010 to 16 million in 2017 (NBS, 2018). Even a majority of those

---

[3] *The administration of President Buhari has introduced some social security programmes including the Homegrown School Feeding Programme that benefits over 8 million school pupils; the Conditional Cash Transfer (CCT) with 297,973 beneficiaries who are the poorest and vulnerable households that receives N5000 monthly, the N-Power Programme, TraderMoni, which is a programme where the Federal government provides N10,000 non-collateral loan to petty traders (2 million petty traders are expected to benefit from the programme), etc. However, there is a problem of sustainability as successive administrations discontinue programmes that their predecessors started. However, if these programmes are sustained in the medium to long term, their development impacts will be reflected in development indicators.*

employed can be termed "working poor", as most of them work in the informal and agricultural sectors.

To illustrate this point, in the third quarter of 2017 for which we have most recent data, Nigeria had a labour force of 85.08 million, of which 77.55 million were engaged in some sort of economic activity. Of this, only 51.06 million, that is 65.84%, worked full time, that is forty hours and above, a week. In effect, 34.16% of those who work are underemployed (NBS, 2018). The problem is more acute when one considers the fact that a number of Nigerians take jobs for which they are overqualified. Underemployment in the agricultural sector is partly due to the seasonal nature of employment in the sector. Most farmers depend on rainfall because irrigation systems remain underdeveloped in the country. As a result, most farmers are unable to engage in undisrupted farming throughout the year. This situation has worsened due to the impact of climate change, such as desertification, drought and flooding.

In the same period, out of those who work full time, 33.80 million or 66.33% are self-employed working in agriculture, while 18.85 million, that is 36%, work in non-agriculture related activities. Nigerians who work for pay/wages constitute only 27.62%, that is, 14.10 million of those who work full time. The unemployment crisis is more intriguing when one examines the types of economic activities that the 77.55 million people in the labour force are engaged in. As the NBS data shows, 38.24% (29.66 million) are self-employed in farming/agriculture, while 27.93% (21.66 million) are self-employed in non-farming/agriculture. This shows that 57.59% of all those who are engaged in economic activities in the country are self-employed and are in the informal sector.

The service sector, especially those in high end services such as ICT and financial services, are not creating enough jobs. While the values of these two sub-sectors have significantly increased in the 18 years (2000–2017) for which data is available, their contribution to employment remained very low. In the third quarter of 2017, ICT

Nigeria: Democracy without Development. How to fix it

30

contributed 0.56% (386,321.84) to total employment figures while financial services employed only 1,016,998 people, representing 1.47% out of the 69,090,007 total employed (NBS, 2018).

Though still low, the creative industry contribution – Nollywood and the music sector – is making significant contributions to both GDP (1.42%) and employment. For instance, Nollywood was responsible for 300,000 direct jobs and one million indirect jobs in 2017 (Kapoor, *et al.*, 2019). However, most of these were not decent and sustainable jobs partly due to the low value addition of the subsector.

We can reach some conclusions from this data. Firstly, the Nigerian economy is characterised by inadequate productive employment and income-generating opportunities. Secondly, as the data on sub-Saharan Africa, including Nigeria, shows a majority of the self-employed live on less than $1.25 dollars a day. In effect, a majority of those employed in Nigeria are the "working poor". Lastly, the economic growth in the democratic dispensation has been a jobless growth.

As shown in Figure 5 below, the unemployment rate in Nigeria has fluctuated over the democratic dispensation (2000 – 2017). In 2000, the unemployment rate was 13.1% and it increased from 14.9% in 2008 to 19.7% in 2009, then there was a general fluctuation between 2010 and 2014, before it began to increase again from 10.44% in 2015 to 18.8% in 2017. Thus, Nigeria in the era of democracy in the last two decades has been characterised by the problems of unemployment and underemployment.

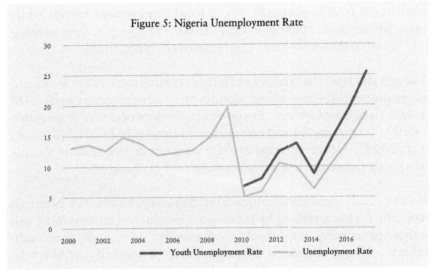

Figure 5: Nigeria Unemployment Rate

Source: NBS 2018

The Problem of Youth Unemployment in the Democratic Era

There are also generational and gender dimensions to the crisis of underemployment and unemployment in the country, as young people are most adversely affected. As shown in Figure 5, in 2011, the percentage of youths (between the ages of 15 and 34) who were unemployed was 8.04%, compared to a general unemployment rate of 5.96%. By 2017, the percentage of youth unemployment increased to 25.48% compared to the general unemployment of 18.80%. It also needs to be noted that the Nigerian economy is unable to absorb new entrants into the labour market, which affects mostly the youths. This situation has given rise to the crisis of graduate unemployment.

In a survey conducted by a recruitment company, jobberman.com, among 89,755 graduates, 41,032 (45.72%) responded that they were unemployed (cited in Sahara Reporters, 2016a). This is consistent with NBS data that shows that unemployment and underemployment are higher amongst those with post-secondary school qualifications –

Nigeria: Democracy without Development. How to fix it

32

50% in the third quarter of 2017 (NBS, 2017b). Quite clearly, the country faces a crisis of graduate unemployment.

Youth unemployment is worsened by the fact that there is no systematic policy and support by the government for the youth to be entrepreneurial: up to 70% of employed graduates are in paid employment. In turn, this points to obsolete university curricula that emphasises paid employment rather than entrepreneurship. It is even worse that the Nigerian higher education system produces "certificated" not "educated" graduates, as most lack the knowledge, skills and competencies required to engage in productive economic activities and to become active citizens, including in civic affairs.

Unemployment by Gender

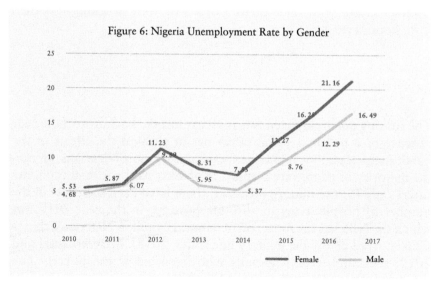

Figure 6: Nigeria Unemployment Rate by Gender

Source: NBS 2018

For the period between 2010 and 2017, for which we have data, as can be seen in Figure 6, unemployment has consistently been more prevalent among females than males. In 2010, the unemployment rate among females was 5.53% and increased to 21.16% in 2017. In contrast, the unemployment rate among males was 4.48% in 2010 and it increased to 16.49% in 2017.

Similarly, females are more disproportionately affected by unemployment and underemployment. As an example, in the fourth quarter of 2016, the unemployment rate among females was 16.3% compared to 12.3% among males (NBS, 2017a). Similarly, more females than males were underemployed in the same period (third quarter of 2017b). Out of the 24.5 million females that were in full-time jobs and underemployed, those unemployed were 33.86%. In contrast, out of the 44.57 million males that worked full time and underemployed, only 12.85% were underemployed (NBS, 2018). In effect, underemployment is more prevalent among females, which means that more females than males were working in jobs not commensurate with their qualifications or were working less than forty hours a week.

Poverty and Inequality

The soaring unemployment rate is set against the backdrop of the near absence of a national social safety net to cushion the effects of the harsh socio-economic realities experienced by most Nigerians. Hence, the majority of people are trapped in poverty as the formal economy caters only for the minority. In fact, there have been increases in the number of people living in absolute poverty. In the year 2010, for which the NBS has the most recent data, 112 million Nigerians, that is 62.6%, lived below the poverty line (NBS, 2018). Between 2004 and 2010, the number of Nigerians who lived below the poverty line increased from 69 million to 112 million. According to Oxfam calculations, $24 billion would be required to lift these people out of poverty, which is less than the $29.9 billion that is the total wealth of the five richest Nigerians (Oxfam, 2017). This reflects the non-

Nigeria: Democracy without Development. How to fix it

34

inclusiveness of the Nigerian economy in the democratic era.

Furthermore, because the formal sector absorbed only a small number of people, there have been increases in inequality. Nigeria's Gini Coefficient has consistently increased since 2000. Its Gini Index increased from 0.40 in 2006 to 0.49 in 2013 (UNDP, 2013; World Bank, 2018c). This is an extraordinary increase, given the high inelasticity of the income Gini Index, which means that inequality does not increase much over time.

The skewed nature of income and wealth in the twenty-first century has not only disempowered the majority of Nigerian citizens, it has also disenfranchised them. Since 1999 there have been cases recorded where citizens sell their votes for small amounts of food items like rice and sugar, or in exchange for money. Thus in Nigeria, democracy does not give the weak the same chance as the strong, as envisioned by one of the iconic figures of the twentieth century, Mahatma Ghandi. The economy is rigged against a majority of its people. Poverty and inequality are two of the major threats to democracy in the country and its growth potential. The poverty rate in the country, that is those that live below $1.90 a day, is 53.5% according to World Bank estimates.

The situation is even bleaker because, by early 2018, according to three researchers of the Brookings Institute, Homi Kharas, Kristofer Hamel and Martin Hofer (2018), Nigeria, which is Africa's largest economy, had overtaken India to become the world's poverty capital with the highest number of people living in extreme poverty. According to their report:

> Nigeria has already overtaken India as the country with the largest number of extreme poor in early 2018, ... At the end of May 2018, our trajectories suggest that Nigeria had about 87 million people in extreme poverty, compared with India's 73 million. What is more, extreme poverty in Nigeria is growing by six people every minute, while poverty in India continues to

fall (Kharas, Hamel, Hofer, 2018).

Though the Nigerian middle class has grown in the Fourth Republic, it remains relatively small in size. For example, in the years for which data is available in the twenty-first century, only 7.9% of Nigerians are in the upper middle-income bracket, which live on more than $5.5 a day or $165 (₦60,000) a month (World Bank, 2017). Put differently, 92.1% Nigerians live on less than $5.5 a day. This is one of the worst records in the world.

Food Insecurity

Chronic food insecurity or undernourishment is another area to examine with respect to the development outcome of democracy in Nigeria. Its reduction is one of the goals of the Sustainable Development Goals (Goal 2, Target 2.2), which calls for an end to all forms of malnutrition by 2030. According to the Food and Agriculture Organisation (FAO) of the United Nations (2017a), globally, there has been a general decline of undernourishment or people living in extreme hunger in the new millennium, from 14.7% in 2000 to 11% in 2016. As a whole, the African continent continued to have the highest rate of undernourished people at 20% in 2016 (declining from 24.3% in 2000).

Unfortunately, Nigeria's undernourished population increased from 6.6% between 2004 and 2006 to 7.9% between 2014 and 2016' therefore bucking the global and continental trend of the declining prevalence of undernourished people. In absolute terms, the number of undernourished people increased from 9.2 million between 2004 and 2006 to 14.3 million people between 2014 and 2016. Like the rest of the world, the problem of food insecurity in Nigeria affects more women than men.

Nigeria: Democracy without Development. How to fix it

36

Furthermore, anaemia, which is an "indicator of both poor nutrition and poverty" remained a major problem across the globe between 2005 and 2016. It decreased slightly from 42% in 2005 to 38% in 2016. In Nigeria, the prevailing rate of anaemia among women between the ages of 15 and 49 years decreased from 52.2% in 2005 to 49.8% in 2016. But this is still exceptionally high, and it is above the continental average (38%).

High Maternal Mortality Rate and Stunted Growth among Children

Maternal mortality rate is a key social indicator for measuring development outcomes. This much is recognised by international development agencies such as the World Bank and the United Nations Development Programme (UNDP).

Table 1 (the next page) shows the twenty-one countries in the world with the highest maternal mortality rates, with more than 500 deaths per 100,000. It shows that Nigeria has the fourth largest maternal mortality rate in the world. Though the maternal mortality rate declined from 1,170 per 100,000 in 2000 to 814 in 2015,[4] it is still higher than war-ravaged Afghanistan with 396 maternal deaths per 100,000 live births in 2015. Also, the decline in the Nigerian mortality rate (from 1170 to 814) is more sluggish than in Afghanistan (1180 in 2000 to 396 in 2015).

All of the above point to the fact that Nigeria is not experiencing inclusive development. Worse still, children are most adversely affected by this phenomenon. While globally, between 2005 and 2016, the rate of stunted growth among children under the age of five declined, the rate remained extremely high in Nigeria as about one in every three children is affected by stunted growth due to undernourishment. Stunting among children under five years in the

[4] *The NBS data is different from that of UNICEF, which shows that maternal mortality rate declined from 800 in 2004 to 243 in 2015 per 100,000. We have used the UNICEF data for purposes of comparison.*

Table 1: Trends in the Maternal Mortality Ratio (maternal deaths per 100,000 live births) 2000 – 2015

Countries/Regions	2000	2005	2010	2015
Angola	924	705	561	477
Burundi	954	863	808	712
Cameroon	750	729	676	596
Central African Republic	1200	1060	909	882
Chad	1370	1170	1040	856
Cote d'Ivoire	671	742	717	645
Democratic Republic of the Congo	874	787	794	693
Eritrea	733	619	579	501
Gambia	887	807	753	706
Guinea	976	831	720	679
Guinea-Bissau	800	714	570	549
Kenya	759	728	605	510
Liberia	1270	1020	811	725
Malawi	890	648	629	634
Mali	834	714	630	587
Mauritania	813	750	723	602
Niger	794	723	657	553
Nigeria	1170	946	867	814
Rwanda	1020	567	381	290
Sierra Leone	2650	1990	1630	1360
Somalia	1080	939	820	732
South Sudan	1310	1090	876	789

Source: UNICEF, 2015

Nigeria: Democracy without Development. How to fix it

38

country declined from 43% in 2005 to 32.9% in 2016, which is still slightly above the continental average of 31.2% (FAO, 2017a).

Low Investment in Education

Nigeria has a young population. About 60% of its population of 194 million is below the age of 25 years. But during the democratic dispensation, Nigeria has consistently underinvested in education, below the 26% recommended by UNESCO. In the 2018 budget, the Federal Government allocated only ₦102.907 billion, that is 7% of its spending, to education. This points to the fact that the Nigerian state is not investing enough in its people. The 2018 education budget is lower than the ₦139.5 billion allocated to the National Assembly, an arm of government whose budgetary spending has remained opaque since 1999, and whose members are among the highest paid legislators in the world.

The education sector is also underfunded in most states in the country, with the exception of a few such as Kaduna State under Governor Nasir Ahmad El-Rufai that allocated over 30% of its budget to education in the last three years. It is therefore no surprise that Nigeria has the largest number of out-of-school children in the world. An estimated 13.2 million Nigerian children were out of school in 2018. A disturbing trend is that since 1999, the number of out-of-school children has been on the increase from 7.1 million in 1999 to 13.2 million in 2018, the highest in the world. Again, Nigeria is now the world capital of out-of-school children.

There is both gender and spatial dimensions to the crisis of out-of-school children in the country because 60% of these children are girls. Also, the phenomenon is more prevalent in the North (60%), with the highest rate in the North East geo-political zone. About 60% of these are young girls. The crisis in the education sector is also evident by the problem of unqualified teachers. In 2013, only 24% of language teachers and 31% of maths teachers achieved 80% on tests that were meant for ten year old children, that is primary four pupils (World Bank, 2018). In 2017, in Kaduna State, of the 33,000 primary school teachers, 66% (21, 780) failed to pass a competency test meant for primary four pupils.

Another problem facing the education sector in the country is that of absenteeism of teachers. According to the World Bank report referred to above, about 25% of teachers were absent from the classes they were meant to be teaching. These absences lead to poor learning outcomes. The educational crisis in Nigeria is also prevalent in the higher education sector. It faces the crisis of poor funding, inadequate and dilapidating infrastructure, poor governance and management, outdated curriculum, inadequate and, at times, unqualified academics, and so on. The eloquent description of the crisis of the African education system, by one of Nigerian leading bloggers, social media entrepreneur and author, Japheth Omojuwa is germane for the Nigerian situation. According to Omojuwa in his book titled, *Digital: the New Code of Wealth*, the "school curriculum continues to look to the past than to the future ... Our schools are essentially providing answers to old questions when the economy is asking new questions" (Omojuwa, 2019: 41).

At a time when countries like Singapore are introducing Coding as a subject in primary schools, the Nigerian education system is still stuck in analogue. In some instances, pupils study under trees or sit on the bare floor due to lack of classrooms and furniture. The poor state of public primary and secondary schools reflects the poor leadership of local government chairmen and governors since these levels of schooling are the responsibilities of local and state governments. One outcome of this poor state of the education system is the problem of graduate unemployment and employablity, as well as the general lack of skills necessary to engage in productive economic activities. Commenting on the problem of underfunding of education in Nigeria, Mba observed that:

the potential dangers of not increasing investment in education are particularly worrying and far-reaching. Nigeria's population growth offers an enormous opportunity if harnessed, but a ticking time bomb if not. Rather than driving the country to new heights, an untrained and under-employed young population could lead the country down the path of social unrest, political instability and economic ruin (Mba, 2018: 2).

Implications of Exclusionary Social and Economic Outcomes on Democracy

In light of the development outcomes discussed above, it can be argued that Nigerian democracy is exclusionary, and it is therefore fragile. While it allowed for political parties to have a semblance of political competition, democratic governments in the Fourth Republic have not been able to incorporate or respond to the demands of the majority of the people in any meaningful way. Consequently, the country is currently ranked 152 out of 157 countries in the Human Development Indicators (HDI) of the World Bank. This is a classic case of what Abrahamsen (2000) termed exclusionary democracy.

It has been shown in several scholarly works that the survival of democracy is dependent on its ability to make credible commitments and incorporate the needs of the poor (Boix, 2003). That democracy in Nigeria is unable to incorporate the needs of the poor and create equal opportunities for all, imperils its future. The trust deficit in Nigeria's democracy is a result of the fact that a majority of Nigerians have not enjoyed democratic dividends while in sharp contrast, elected officials, senior bureaucrats and their patrons live in affluence. The poor development outcomes of democracy in the country is making millions of Nigerians – including women, youth and other marginalised groups – to question democracy, thus eroding its legitimacy and credibility. The analysis in this book demonstrates that rising poverty, inequality and unemployment undermines the credibility of liberal democracy among the people. This is not to suggest that Nigerians yearn for a return to military rule, but to show their unhappiness and to express their dashed hopes about the social and economic outcomes of democracy. Their unhappiness is further compounded by rampant corruption by the political class and their cronies. In an apt editorial, one of the most respected newspapers in the country, *The Guardian* (2018) observed that:

> ... the public is disenchanted with the political class. There is hardly any redeeming feature in their engagement with the polity. The average Nigerian now sees politicians as a bunch of indulgent fat cats feeding on the national patrimony without anything to show for taxpayers' funds they daily waste on only themselves.

This chapter has described the development deficits in Nigeria since 1999. This is exemplified by the fact that Nigeria was one of the countries that failed to meet most of the targets of the Millennium Development Goals (MDGs). According to the International Labour Organisation (ILO), the problem "is that economic growth is not inclusive enough, excluding millions from the dignity of work, exacerbating inequalities and ultimately narrowing the foundations for sustainable development" (ILO, 2015: 6).

On the basis of the empirical evidence shown above, we can conclude that successive administrations in the democratic dispensation have not only been unable to transform the structure of the economy but have also fostered a non-inclusive socio-economic outcome. In addition, the democratic dispensation has not boosted social justice and has failed to improve the wellbeing of a majority of Nigerians.

In fact, twenty years of democracy has witnessed the paradox of high levels of poverty, inequality and unemployment in the midst of high economic growth, and therefore denies Nigerians the right to being human. Former South African president, Nelson Mandela provides

Nigeria: Democracy without Development. How to fix it

42

insight on the implications of this when he observed that:

> The very right to be human is denied every day to hundreds of
> millions of people as a result of poverty, the unavailability of
> basic necessities such as food, jobs, water and shelter,
> education, health care and a healthy environment. (Mandela,
> 1998).

The paradox of liberal democracy is observable across the African
continent. The United Nations Research Institute for Social
Development (UNRISD), captured it thus:

> If the protests in many African countries that saw the end of
> the authoritarian single-party state and military rule were
> triggered by mass entitlement failures imposed by the
> orthodox stabilization policies of the 1990s, the electoral
> polity that emerged in the aftermath has not ensured the
> flourishing of human well-being, significant reduction in
> poverty, declining wealth inequality, and better employment.
> Such is the paradox of liberal democracy in much of Africa
> since the 1990s (UNRISD, 2019: 1).

Under the democratic era, the Nigerian economy has worked for the
wealthy few and not for all Nigerians, most of whom live below the
poverty line. It is in this context that we should understand the culture
whereby some voters see election season as a "time of harvest" by
collecting money from candidates before they vote. In Nigeria, the
political system is transactional among politicians on the one hand
and transactional between politicians and voters on the other hand.

In the next chapter the institutional factors that explain why Nigerian
democracy has not been able to engender developmentalism and
democratic governance will be examined. Put differently, what are the
factors that explain the paradoxical relationship between liberal
democracy and development in Nigeria?

Chapter Three

Nigerian Political Leadership: The Lack of Ideology of Development Nationalism and Valueless Politics

Introduction

Nigeria is endowed with enormous human and natural resources, which if properly harnessed, could make it one of the most developed countries in the world. But the country remains undeveloped. It is a rich country with poor people; a situation of poverty in the midst of plenty.

Why have some nations developed, and others have not? Nations develop because patriotic individuals come together to transform their societies based on an objective assessment of the material conditions of such a country in an effort at national survival. This shows that leadership is a key driver for a country's progress - nations rise or fall by the nature of their leadership. This situational imperative constitutes the basis of the ideological orientation of the political elite. Indeed, the ideological orientation adopted by the elite to overcome developmental challenges of their country is both contextual and historically contingent. But the common trend is that the elite come together to overcome the challenges of underdevelopment, and to ensure the progress and prosperity of their nation and people.

One of the most reform-minded politicians of the Fourth Republic in Nigeria and current governor of Kaduna State, Nasir Ahmad el-Rufai captured it thus:

> Societies make progress when visionary leaders emerge to organize and direct collective actions for peaceful coexistence, with sensible rules, clear incentives and sanctions that enable individuals to realize their full potential (El-Rufai, 2010: 2).

These leaders possess the ideology of development nationalism, which becomes the major impetus for national development.

Some of the key characteristics of these leaders include being visionary; intelligent; having the ability and courage to put their principles into actions; to listen and work collaboratively with other actors, within and outside the state; to deal with complex and consequential problems; to empathise with citizens and; to put national interests above personal and parochial interests.

The main source of political capacity is a political leadership that is transformational. Based on this ideological orientation, these leaders not only articulate a development agenda which they foist on society, but they establish both the administrative and technical capacities to achieve their goals for transformation. In celebrated developmental states such as Japan, South Korea, Singapore, Malaysia and Mauritius

Nigeria: Democracy without Development. How to fix it

46

(the only developmental state in Africa), the political elite constructed what Chalmers Johnson (1982) calls plan rationale states and developed transformative institutional capacity. It is the institutional capacity that enables the state to promote effective policy coordination, implementation, monitoring and evaluation (Weiss, 2010). The central policy objectives are strategic industrial development and human capital expansion. Development planning has been a central mechanism used by the developmentalist elite to promote transformational change.

As we will see in this chapter, it is evident that the political elite in the twenty years of Nigeria's Fourth Republic are not developmentalist but rent-seeking and predatory. I opined that Nigeria's social, economic and political crisis are primarily attributed to the absence of both a coalition of developmentalist elites and a broad Developmentalist Coalition (DC) in the groups that took state power since 1999. To develop and to create a shared future, I argue in this chapter for the need to set up a coalition of like-minded people who are driven by the ideology of development nationalism. The coalition has to be united mainly by the need to create wealth and make Nigeria and its people prosper.

The objective conditions in the country including robbery, banditry and kidnapping, the rise of ethnic militias, terrorism, the menace of murderous herdsmen, and ethnic and religious conflicts, are potent reasons for a developmentalist elite to form a DC in the country. Other factors are high levels of poverty, unemployment and inequality; poor management of the economy; and the inability of the political leadership to transform its structure; endemic corruption and state capture; mismanagement of public resources; and poor governance and dysfunctional state institutions. This much is supported by the development literature that points to the fact that internal or external threats could force developmental leadership to form coalitions to address collective action problems (Leftwich, 2010).

47

Nigeria: Democracy without Development. How to fix it

Unless developmentalists in Nigeria come together to form a coalition to rescue the country and ensure that democracy delivers development dividends to citizens, constitutional democracy will remain threatened. Such a coalition will have to work in concert with citizens to address the structural injustices that have deprived a majority of Nigerians from enjoying the benefits of democracy.

Developmental Leadership: Concepts and Experiences from Other Contexts

The importance of leadership to economic development has been eloquently captured thus:

> Economic progress depends to a large extent upon the adoption by governments of appropriate administrative and legislative action...we wish to emphasize that the masses of the people take their cue from those who are in authority over them. If the leaders are reactionary, selfish and corrupt, the masses in turn are dispirited, and seem to lack initiative. But if the leaders win the confidence of the country, and prove themselves vigorous in eradicating privilege and gross inequalities, they can inspire the masses with an enthusiasm for progress which carries all before it...all problems of economic development are soluble (United Nations Department of Economic Affairs, 1951: 16 - 17).

In the context of developmental states, a developmental leadership emerges and becomes the dominant leaders in society. According to Leftwich:

> Developmental leadership is an inherently political process involving the organisation and mobilisation of people and resources in pursuit of particular goals, in given institutional context of authority, legitimacy and power...Achieving these

Nigeria: Democracy without Development. How to fix it

48

goals, and overcoming the collective action problems which commonly obstruct their achievement, normally requires negotiating locally appropriate institutions by formal or informal coalitions of interests, elites and organisations, both vertical and horizontal (Leftwich, 2010: 103).

In developmental states, this leadership is driven by an ideology of "development nationalism" – the need to catch up and to overcome underdevelopment. In effect, it is an ideology premised on the need to address the challenges of growth, human capital development and wellbeing. In general, these leaders exhibit the characteristics of ethical and moral leadership, honesty and efficiency. These characteristics make it possible to gain the trust of their people. Nationalistic/patriotic political leaders such as the founding Prime Minister of Singapore, Mr Lee Kuan Yew and Prime Minister Mahattir Mohamad of Malaysia, were able to foster a hegemonic developmentalist ideology on society and build the necessary coalitions to underpin it. The same is true of the Scandinavian social democratic leadership, as well as the developmentalists of the East Asian[5] developmental states.

Throughout history, the ideology of development nationalism has been a major impetus for national development, especially in late developers (such as China, Malaysia, Mauritius, South Korea, Singapore and more recently the United Arab Emirates) that want to "catch up". Development is therefore the material base of the ideology of nationalism, and nationalism as ideology serves as both a means of promoting development as well as coping with development. Developmental nationalism, in this sense, is a commitment to make one's country progress and prosper, including the development of the capacities of its people to fulfil their potential and serve as drivers of the desired development. This ideology is promoted by patriotic elites. The definition of elite by Leftwich is germane for our purpose.

---

[5] Note that though some of the East Asian states such as South Korea started as an authoritarian developmental state, there was subsequent recognition that authoritarian developmental states were unsustainable in the long-run, hence the need to transition to a democratic developmental state. See Kim (2010) for elaboration on this in South Korea.

49

Nigeria: Democracy without Development. How to fix it

According to him, "Elites consist of a small group of leaders...occupying formal and informal positions of authority and power in public and private organisations or sectors and who take or influence key economic, political, social and administrative decisions" (Leftwich, 2010: 104).

To developmental elites, the ideology of development nationalism trumps other considerations and identities. They love their countries and people. These elites are primarily driven by developmentalism—to overcome underdevelopment and dependence on foreign countries, as well as to improve the living standards of their people. As the Vice President and Prime Minister of the United Arab Emirates who has been one of the main architects of the remarkable development of Dubai, Sheik Mohammed bin Rashid Al Maktoum (2012) puts it, such leadership has a clear developmentalist vision that includes the improvement of the status of their people and assembling a competent executive and technocratic team to ensure the vision is implementable and the developmental goals are achieved. They see underdevelopment, dependence on foreign countries and poverty as threats to not only national survival but also to their enlightened self-interest. Enhancing the productive capacity of their country is the main preoccupation of such a developmentalist elite. This entails massive investment in human capital development (education and training, health and other social services) and infrastructure including roads, rails and communications, as well as promoting industrialisation. Cognizant of the fact that they cannot achieve these goals on their own, developmental elites form coalitions. As Leftwich puts it, they are "developmentally positive in helping to organize the fundamental agreements, politics and institutional arrangements without which growth, stability and inclusive development is impossible" (Leftwich, 2010: 106).

Developmental elites strive to establish inclusive economic and political institutions to actualise their goals, which they could not achieve individually. They do not engage in the politics of self-enrichment that will undermine the collective national interest; rather,

Nigeria: Democracy without Development. How to fix it

50

they make necessary sacrifices to achieve their collective goals.

Reflecting on the developmental states of East Asia, Chalmers Johnson (1987), who coined the term "developmental state" to describe the role of the state in Asian developmental success, observed that the DCs in East Asian countries were "generated and came to the fore because of the desire to break out of the stagnation of dependency and underdevelopment; the truly successful ones understand that they need the market to maintain efficiency, motivate the people over the long term, and serve as a check on institutionalised corruption while battling against underdevelopment." Such an elite, and a DC, "is not committed first and foremost to the enhancement and perpetuation of its *elites' privileges but to the long-term development of their societies*" (Johnson, 1987: 140, *emphasis added*).

Generally, developmentalist elites have a shared vision for national development. They are cognizant of the fact that the realisation of their vision is dependent on their ability to enhance the productive capacities of their economies and people. Wealth creation, thus production/value addition rather than consumption/rent-seeking, is the major preoccupation of a coalition of developmentalist elites, as well as a broad developmentalist coalition. Both are conscious of the fact that private gains must be compatible with social objectives. Human capital development, and ultimately human wellbeing, is thus one of their main priorities.

A coalition of developmentalist elites ensure that over time the ideology of developmentalism becomes a national culture. Through words and actions, they mobilise citizens to buy into its agenda. More importantly, it ensures that its agenda is anchored on a social base, hence the developmental elites identify social groups with which to form a broad DC. When developmentalists occupy political positions, they use their positions to ensure that all segments of society make short-term economic sacrifices for long-term shared prosperity.

As a consequence, all the sectors of society avoid, or at least minimise, rent-seeking behaviour for the sake of national development. When such a coalition assumes political power, it undertakes necessary governance and policy reforms to give expression to its vision of development for the country. This is how it creates a society in its own image. In all spheres of society, it provides leadership to ensure outcomes that are compatible with its broad vision.

The political and economic affairs of most developed nations are dominated by DCs in different forms. In some instances, the developmentalist elites might form their own political parties (such as the People's Action Party formed by the first prime minister of Singapore, Lee Kuan Yew and his colleagues) to contest for political power or they might join different political parties. However, in the context where developmentalists are the dominant political elite, whatever party is in power, it ensures that they maintain some minimum standards that are the core principles on which the country is governed. A good example is the Scandinavian countries where the ideology of social democracy was foisted on their societies mainly by trade unions with the support of small farmers. As a result, this ideology has taken root. One outcome of this is that irrespective of the political party in power – whether with left or right political leanings – it ensures that the core principles of social democracy are not compromised. As a consequence, there is predictability in governance, including the rule of law, and the provision of basic public goods to citizens. In the US, the Fourth Amendment (which protects against unreasonable search and seizure) and free markets are foundational and uncompromising principles irrespective of which of the two political parties, Democrat or Republican, is in power. This unity was due to external threats, that is, antagonism from King George of the United Kingdom and British mercantilism.

This is not to suggest that only external threats give rise to a DC. As an example, in Malaysia, the May 1969 protests gave birth to a DC in the country to make UMNO the dominant political party for more than

---

⁶ *UMNO lost the election in 2018 due mainly to the corruption of the Prime Minister, Razak. At the time of writing, he is being prosecuted.*

Nigeria: Democracy without Development. How to fix it

52

forty years[6]. Without the protests that threatened the political survival
of the Bumiputra elite, they would not have bonded as a dominant
political force, and subsequently become important economic actors.
Developmentalist elites articulate values that bind and define their
nations. They provide both moral and political leadership, such as
former President Nelson Mandela of South Africa. Also, most
developmental elites tend to favour the establishment of inclusive
economic and political institutions that enable them achieve their
development objectives.

To attain this goal, these elites reach an informal consensus on the type
of society they want to build. Over time, they foist the developmental
ideology on citizens. This becomes the national ideology and values
that are embraced by citizens irrespective of class, gender, religion,
ethnicity, etc.

In most cases, developmentalism is driven by the need to transform the
structures of the economy and to industrialise as well as build human
capacity. DCs, especially those in control of government – in both
elected and administrative positions – have used their positions to
undertake necessary institutional and policy reforms, in addition to
mobilising citizens to ensure that developmentalism becomes the
hegemonic ideology of the state and society. These are transformative
leaders with a strong desire to effect positive change in their society. To
do this however, requires that development nationalism as an ideology
is embedded in specific social groups, such as trade unions,
entrepreneurs, professional groups, the unemployed, and so on. The
specific social group with which a coalition of developmentalist elites
form an alliance is however, informed by contextual conditions. The
objectives remain the same, namely: enhancement of the productive
capacity and promotion of shared prosperity in an inclusive economy.

It should be noted that development nationalism is informed and
anchored on situational imperatives. Therefore, politics matters in
fostering democratic developmentalism. Through political capacity,
elected officials set the broad development frameworks and create the

institutional architecture – administrative and technical – to achieve the agenda. In turn, the political leadership allows the administrative elite, who are in various professional cadres, to design and deploy the policy tools to achieve the goals the former has set forth with limited interference.

In general, political leaders set the broad development agenda, while the administrative leaders devise and deploy the policy tools toward its attainment. Thus, political leaders reigned while administrative leaders ruled (Johnson, 1982; 1987). This division of labour is precisely what minimises conflict between the two sets of leaders in the public service and administration[7].

The success of the system and the effectiveness of public officials, as well as state institutions, are dependent on the political leadership supporting the strategic policy choices taken by bureaucrats. This means that political leaders do not unnecessarily interfere with the work of administrative leaders. Crucially, the political system has to be such that bureaucrats are insulated (not isolated) from direct political pressure. Deyo points to the positive impact of insulation of bureaucrats from direct political pressure by sectional interests. According to him, where political leaders insulate state technocrats from domestic pressures, they will be relatively free to employ largely technical and economic criteria in development planning (Deyo, 1992: 234 cited in Public Service Commission, 2014a). Insulation contributes to the state's autonomy because the political system is such that it gives the bureaucracy sufficient scope to take initiative and operate effectively. In Johnson's view:

> This means, concretely, that the legislative and judicial branches of government must be restricted to "safety valve" functions. These two branches of government must stand ready to intervene in the work of the bureaucracy and restrain it when it has gone too far, but their more important overall

---

[7]   *In this and the subsequent two paragraphs, I have drawn on the concept paper on the developmental state that I wrote for the Public Service Commission of South Africa.*

function is to fend off the numerous interest groups in society, which if catered to would distort the priorities of the developmental state. In the case of interests that cannot be ignored, deflected, or satisfied in symbolic ways – or upon which the perpetuation of the political system depends – the political leaders must compel the bureaucracy to serve and manipulate them" (Johnson, 1982: 315 – 316).

This is especially important in a democratic context, as Breslin (1996) observed, because politicians are motivated by seeking popular support in the short term. Therefore, long-term economic strategy must, as far as possible, be insulated from the vagaries of competing political demands which, if acceded to, would undermine national development. As Johnson observed:

> Political leaders attempting to implement long-term industrial development *in particular and national development in general* must therefore have the capacity to depoliticise in part their key economic decisions. This is normally done by entrusting such decisions to a "non-political elite", sheltered to some degree from direct political pressure (Johnson, 1987 cited in Breslin, 1996: 692, *emphasis added*).

The god of Money, Self-Interest and Ideological Poverty of the Nigerian Political Elite

Since independence, Nigeria has had the misfortune of being governed by a political class[8] bereft of the ideology of development nationalism. As a result, the country has witnessed a deterioration in quality of both elected officials and the administrative elite. The social, economic and political crisis in the country can largely be attributed to the absence of

---

[8] *Gaetano Mosca (1939) defined political class as the political and bureaucratic elites.*

a DC that is patriotic and committed to the transformation of the structure of the Nigerian economy in order to overcome underdevelopment. Public affairs, especially politics and the economy, have been dominated by groups that lack a vision on how to transform the country: industrialise it; build common values that unite the people; address poverty and underdevelopment and ethnic and religious divisions. The late iconic Nigerian novelist and critic, Professor Chinua Achebe (1983) rightly captured this in his book entitled, *The Trouble with Nigeria*. According to him, "The trouble with Nigeria is simply a failure of leadership...the Nigerian problem is the unwillingness or inability of its leaders to rise to the responsibility … of true leadership (Achebe, 1983: 1).

The leadership crisis which has worsened since 1999, can be linked to the transition to democracy in the early 1990s during General Ibrahim Babangida's reign. He banned credible politicians and postponed announcing handover dates several times. In the end, he imposed two political parties on the country: the National Republican Convention (NRC) and the Social Democratic Party (SDP). When elections were subsequently held on June 12 1993, Babangida annulled the results of the presidential election that was adjudged by Nigerians and the international community to be the freest and fairest in the history of the country. The winner of the election, Chief M.K.O. Abiola was subsequently arrested and detained by General Sani Abacha. Abiola died in mysterious circumstances in detention.

Following the death of Abacha, General Abdulsalami Abubukar took over the reins of power and his military regime initiated a transition programme, but most credible politicians and activists refused to participate in it due to the perceived lack of credibility. This created a vacuum for two categories of people to dominate Nigeria's politics, and subsequently capture the state: those with a military background, which the erudite political economist, Professor Pat Utomi (2016a) described as the Class of 1966, and those with suspicious backgrounds. As Akinduro and Masterson put it, this is a process where the "captors seek to manipulate this process – electoral process

Nigeria: Democracy without Development. How to fix it

56

– to remove the guarantee of the people's free will by making it an expression of the will of a few, even though an election still takes place to create a façade" (2018: 60).

According to Utomi, the Class of '66 and those they co-opted in the Fourth Republic were neither nation builders nor wealth creators. Their "mindset is kill and share; divide and rule". To them "elections have become wars and public office holders consume resources for infrastructure and growth, in the enjoyment of the perquisites of power". These are a gluttonous political elite. As a consequence, they do not understand that "leadership is other-centred" (Utomi, 2016a: 3–4). In his analysis, these groups are anti-intellectual and are driven by self-interest alone and not by any principled policy agenda (Utomi, 2016b). It is in the light of this that one of Nigeria's most respected voices, the Archbishop Emeritus of the Catholic Archdiocese of Abuja, Cardinal John Onaiyekan (2019a) cautioned that politics and public service should be about service and not the domination of citizens by the political class.

This background is necessary to understand the deteriorating quality of political leadership in the Fourth Republic. As an example, state governors of the Second Republic were more urbane, more visionary and development oriented and less corrupt than those of the Fourth Republic. To illustrate this point, in terms of development outlook, Second Republic governors such as Alhaji Balarabe Musa (Kaduna State), Chief Bola Ige (Oyo State), Prof Ambrose Ali (Bendel State), Alhaji Lateef Jakande (Lagos State) and Sam Mbakwe (Imo State) were more nationalistic and committed to socio-economic development than their successors in the Fourth Republic such as Ayo Fayose (Ekiti State), Ikedi G. Ohakim (Imo State) Ahmad Sani Yarima (Zamfara State), Lucky Igbinedion (Edo State). The same comparison is true of members of the National Assembly and State Houses of Assembly.

Over time, the country has witnessed a gradual deterioration of the quality of elected officials and political appointees. Also, although politics in the country has been corrupt since independence, it became institutionalised by the military regime of General Babangida. This is a legacy he bequeathed to political leaders since 1999. In general, most politicians and top public servants of the Fourth Republic do not appreciate the fact that leadership is about service to their constituents – the former are mostly *political jobbers*. Consequently, Cardinal Onaiyekan lamented that the country's politicians, since 1999, are so desperate that they militarised and rigged elections. According to him, elections were supposed to be a process that enabled voters choose those who governed them but in the Fourth Republic, he argues:

> Elections are supposed to be an opportunity for us to choose those who will serve us. In many cases, it has been turned into a battlefield for warriors to capture power and conquer territory and people. No wonder it has become such a do-or-die affair and winner takes all. No wonder the process has become militarised, with armed thugs engaging security forces, who in turn are rarely able to be as fair and professional as they claim to be (Onaiyekan, 2019b: 1-2).

In the final analysis, he correctly notes that it is the voters who are denied the opportunity to choose who will serve them as political leaders. He was also correct that militarised and rigged elections cannot lead to good governance.

The two dominant political parties in the last twenty years, the People's Democratic Party (PDP) who governed the country from May 1999 to May 2015, and the All Progressives Congress (APC), who took over power from May 2015 till date have no clear cut ideology[9]. This is unlike the political parties of the First and Second Republics, which to a degree were differentiated ideologically. As an example, the National Party of Nigeria (NPN), under which President Shehu

---

[9] *The APC will claim that its ideology is social democracy, and will point to its manifesto as evidence. But the social democratic nature of the party is practiced in the breach. Also, politicians do not join it because of its ideology but because it is a political machine to achieve personal political ambition. It is in this context that its members defect from and re-defect to other political parties, especially the PDP.*

Shagari was elected, was conservative in nature compared to the Unity Party of Nigeria (UPN) led by Chief Obafemi Awolowo that can be described as a social democratic party.

In the absence of an ideologically-oriented party, elections are not based on manifestos but rather on meaningless sloganeering. Those that have occupied political and administrative leadership positions since 1999 have been driven largely by narrow, primordial and personal interests. One of the main challenges facing Nigeria is that political parties are not ideologically driven; rather, they are based on naked ambition for power and wealth accumulation, the latter through the looting of the commonwealth[10]. Political parties are not platforms for any meaningful societal change but mere vehicles for the political class to capture political power. Commenting on the current set of politicians, Reuben Abati (2018), observed:

> ...our politicians are not principled at all. They can belong to the PDP in the morning, the APC by noon and within 24 hours, they could join a completely new party and advance strong arguments to justify their nomadism. The political parties are not built on any concrete principles or ideology either; they are vehicles for political survival and access to power by ambitious politicians.

Nigerian politics in the first two decades of the twenty-first century is devoid of loyalty, honesty, integrity, ideology, principles and intellectualism; politicians are anti-intellectuals. Given this background, public policy is largely not evidence-based. Furthermore, most of the current political parties do not function as organisations. Their members have no common goals they pursue and those in leadership positions are unaccountable to members, hence politicians are undisciplined, and the parties are not cohesive. The political parties are anti-democratic, lack internal democracy and violate most

---

[10] *This explains the defection of politicians from one party to the other. These defections have nothing to do with the interests of citizens but are rather driven by a naked quest for power in order to place themselves in positions to loot the commonwealth.*

principles of good governance.

Godfatherism and The Subversion of Democracy

The absence of internal party democracy is partly due to the phenomenon of "godfatherism", whereby financiers determine who gets party tickets and gets elected, and impose candidates both in the political parties and in elective positions. According to Afe Babalola S.A.N., a leading Nigerian lawyer:

> A godfather in the Nigerian context is one who by virtue of either immense wealth or political goodwill is able to determine not only the persons that are nominated by their parties to contest elections but who in most cases are able to guarantee the victory of such candidates. The said guarantee may come in the form of purchase of votes or outright intimidation of voters and hardly by legitimate means. A political godfather in the Nigerian context may even be able to form and finance a political party (Babalola, 2018).

The "elected" officials, that is the "godsons", are stooges of the godfathers, who were either former senior military officials, traditional rulers, religious leaders, former and current elected officials (including former heads of state, presidents, former and current governors, and so on). The godfathers have an overbearing influence on the polity and governance. Some have created what can be described as dynasties. Some are so powerful that even when in prison, they still influence the political process, including determining who gets into elective positions. A case in point is that of the former governor of Delta State, James Ibori, who according to the Chairman of the PDP, Uche Secondus, from his prison cell in Britain, influenced the emergence of Ifeanyi Okowa as the party's gubernatorial candidate in the state in 2015 (*Punch*, 2018a).

The phenomenon of godfatherism has several negative effects on democracy and development. First, it compromises the recruitment process of elected officials, because merit is jettisoned in the process. The political godsons are not elected because of their leadership qualities, development vision, competencies or acumen[11], but rather because of their ability to repay and enable their benefactors loot state resources. In a poignant critique of godfathers, an Electrical Engineer based in Bauchi State, Kelvin Idoko, interviewed by the *Daily Trust* newspaper observed that "the political problems of mediocrity, incompetence in governance, lack of foresight, and inefficiency" in the era of liberal democracy in the country are attributable to the meddling influence of godfathers (Daily Trust, 2019).

A senior lecturer of Political Science at the University of Lagos, Dr. Dele Ashiru, persuasively argued that "democracy is about the people, but where you have few people taking key decisions such as recruitment of public officials, such a polity cannot be described as democracy and it will not be able to thrive" (BBC News, 2019). Therefore, democracy is endangered by the overbearing role of godfathers.

Secondly, godfatherism encourages corruption in the polity and militates against development because it thrives on transactional politics. Godfathers have turned politics in Nigeria into selling and buying of political power. They sell power to the highest bidders, allowing them to capture and control national resources for their self-interests. The history of corruption in Nigerian politics since 1999 can hardly be written without godfathers occupying a prime place. Resources meant for national development, including those for physical and social infrastructure, are diverted to their private

---

[11] *Some possible exceptions include two former Lagos State Governors, Babatunde Fashola and Akinwunmi Ambode. To his credit, Senator Bola Tinubu groomed them to be among the best performing Governors in the democratic dispensation. Others protégées of Senator Tinubu occupy various leadership positions in the country, including the current Vice President, Prof Yemi Osibanjo, and have been relatively efficient. This is not to suggest that his role as a godfather has not at times been problematic, including his falling out for various reasons with both Fashola and Ambode. But his succession planning and his ability to mentor competent and credible protégées are commendable.*

pockets. In some instances, they fail to execute contracts, yet they are paid by governments. A godfather will take punitive measures against a godson who refuses to pay the former for a non-executed project. This, partly, explains the phenomenon of abandoned projects discussed later in this book.

Thirdly, godfathers impose candidates through violence and inducement of party members and the electorate. This denies voters the right to freely choose who represents them. At times, the imposition of candidates is done in such a brazen manner where the names of candidates who won party primaries are substituted with the godsons of godfathers. An example is Rotimi Amaechi, who won the PDP Rivers State gubernatorial primaries in 2007. His name was substituted by the PDP leadership with another candidate in the general elections due to the alleged influence of the governor of Rivers State, Peter Odili and President Obasanjo, who opposed his candidature. Amaechi became governor following a Supreme Court ruling that he was the authentic PDP candidate for the election.

In its report titled, "Corruption, Godfatherism and the Funding of Political Violence in Nigeria", Human Rights Watch (2007a) shows how godfatherism promotes political violence and corruption. In the report, it notes as follows:

> Godfatherism is both a symptom and a cause of the violence and corruption that together permeates the political process in Nigeria. Public officials who owe their position to the efforts of a political godfather incur a debt they are expected to repay without end throughout their tenure in office. Godfathers are only relevant because politicians are able to deploy violence and corruption with impunity to compete for office in contests that often effectively, and sometimes actually, exclude Nigeria's voters altogether. But their activities also help to reinforce the central role of violence and corruption in politics by making it even more difficult to win elected office without resorting to the illegal tactics they represent (Human Rights

Nigeria: Democracy without Development. How to fix it

62

Watch, 2007a: 2).

The political godfathers hire thugs to ensure that their candidates
"win" elections. Some of these thugs graduate to hardened criminals –
robbers, kidnappers, bandits and terrorists. This phenomenon was
perfected and institutionalised by the PDP that governed the country
for sixteen years from May 1999 to May 2015. The rigging of
elections and its accompanying violence was so bad that President
Umaru Yar'Adua acknowledged in his inaugural address that the
election through which he emerged as president was flawed.

Fourthly, godfathers are a source of instability in the political system
and they have undermined the democratic order. If a godson tries to
exert some level of independence, the godfather would engineer
his/her removal from office (through legal and illegal means). An
example is the case of former governor of Anambra State, Chris Ngige
who reneged on his agreement with his godfather, Chris Uba who had
allegedly bankrolled his election with the sum of three billion naira.

As reported by Human Rights Watch (2007b), Ngige promised to
"exercise and manifest absolute loyalty to the person of Chief Chris
Uba as my mentor, benefactor and sponsor and agree to allow Uba
control over all important government appointments and the
awarding of all government contracts". When he reneged on this
agreement, Ngige was kidnapped and forced to sign a resignation
letter by armed policemen on the alleged instruction of Uba and the
Federal Government under President Obasanjo in July 2003.

In other instances, the godfathers ensured that their "wayward" and
"disloyal" godsons did not get a party ticket for re-election. For
example, the then governor of Anambra State, Chinwoke Mbadinuju
(1999 – 2003) lost the PDP gubernatorial ticket in 2003 due to the
disagreement with his godfather, Emeka Offor (Chukwuemeka et al.,
n.d). There is the general perception that Governor Akinwunmi
Ambode of Lagos State lost the APC gubernatorial primaries in 2018
due to his fall-out with his godfather, Senator Bola Tinubu, who not

only holds sway over the party in the state but is also the national leader of the party.

Conflicts between godfathers and godsons have been one of the dominant trends in the polity since 1999, such as that between former governor of Kano State, Senator Rabiu Kwankwaso and his former deputy and successor, Governor Abdullahi Umar Ganduje, as well as between former governor of Akwa Ibom State, Senator Godswill Akpabio and his successor, Governor Udom Gabriel Emmanuel.

At the time of concluding this book in July 2019, there is currently a raging crisis between former governor of Edo State and the current National Chairman of the APC, Adams Oshiomhole and his successor and godson, Governor Godwin Obaseki. This crisis has spilled over to the state House of Assembly. Governor Obaseki has attributed the crisis to his refusal "to share state money with godfathers" (Obaseki, 2019a). But there seems to be more to the acrimonious relationship between Oshiomhole and Obaseki. In an audio interview circulated on social media, Obaseki admitted that he was unhappy with his former ally because he had not been able to nominate any candidate for appointment at the federal level. Suffice it to say that similar conflicting relationships exist between governors and members of the legislative arm at the federal and state levels. When there is a fall-out, governors ensure that the erring legislators do not win party primaries.

All of the above have polarized and increased the level of divisions in political parties in the country. In the end, it is ordinary citizens and the country that suffer from the in-fighting between godfathers and their beneficiaries. Thus, as Babalola correctly argued:

> ...the citizenry will end up being impoverished due to the fact that a leadership that is totally disconnected from the aspirations of the people has been produced by a flawed system. In addition to the above, society suffers in several other ways from the concept of godfatherism in the form of

Nigeria: Democracy without Development. How to fix it

64

increased crime rate and a general lack of respect for the due
process of law (Babalola, 2018: 1).

Lack of Internal Democracy and Commercialisation of Party Tickets

Democracy in the Fourth Republic is undermined partly by an absence
of internal democracy within political parties. Party primaries for
elective positions are routinely hijacked by the highest bidders and
party tickets are handed to the favourites of party leaders. As an
example, most of the 3,274 accredited delegates at the PDP elective
convention (where its presidential candidate emerged in 2018) were
reported to have received $9,000 as bribes to vote for particular
candidates (*Punch*, 2018b) and this has been the trend since 1999.
There are even more brazen cases. Ahmed Gulak, chairman of the
panel that oversaw the governorship primaries of the All Progressives
Congress (APC) in Imo State, alleged that the camp of one of the
aspirants offered him two million dollars ($2m) as a bribe to
manipulate the 2018 party primaries in favour of their candidate. He
also claimed there was an attempt to kidnap him to declare the result
in favour of that candidate (*The Cable*, 2018).

In some instances, in the 2018 primaries, across political parties,
primaries did not hold. The Independent National Electoral
Commission (INEC) refused to register candidates of the APC in
Zamfara State because they were not products of party primaries and
this was the reason why the party could not field candidates for some
elective offices in 2019. Although the electoral body changed its
position because of a court ruling, and the party was declared the
winner of most of the positions – including the position of governor –
the Court of Appeal finally backed the original position of INEC and
the party was adjudged to have wrongly participated in the election.

65

Nigeria: Democracy without Development. How to fix it

Even in some states where party primaries took place, the rules of the game were twisted, and names of delegates were not made available to the aspirants, such as during the APC governorship primaries in Delta State. Political parties' primaries are often rigged. Officials sent from the national headquarters to superintend the primaries are usually instructed to achieve a particular outcome by all means. In the process, all norms and rules are subverted in spite of objections by delegates and some aspirants. Parties' primaries for elective positions have become one means that the political class routinely use to subvert the democratic process since 1999.

Courts are consequently invalidating some of the political party primaries in some states. Suffice it to mention two cases here, namely the primary elections of the APC in Rivers State and the aforementioned case of the APC in Zamfara State. In both cases, the Supreme Court ruled that primaries were not conducted. While invalidating the APC primary in Zamfara State, the Supreme Court declared the PDP – whose candidates lost the General Elections – winners of positions ranging from governor, senators, members of the House of Representatives to members of the State House of Assembly. In its ruling, the Supreme Court on May 24, 2019 noted that, the APC "could not have won the elections since it had no valid candidates in the said polls" (see PremiumTimes, 2019a). It therefore declared candidates of the PDP, which had the second highest number of votes, as the winners.

Similarly, in Rivers State, the APC did not field candidates for the governorship, senate, House of Representatives and state House of Assembly because the courts ruled that the party did not conduct party primaries as prescribed by the rules of the party and in accordance with the guidelines of INEC. The lack of transparent guidelines – or their violations where they exist – for political parties' primaries is one of the main factors that has undermined and eroded the credibility of electoral democracy in Nigeria since 1999. It should also be noted that other political parties primaries, including the PDP primaries, witnessed their fair share of controversies.

Nigeria: Democracy without Development. How to fix it

66

In general, the electoral process has been commercialised and corrupted, and this has compromised the integrity of the democratic process. Lamenting on the corrupting influence of money on democracy, President Muhammadu Buhari observed that:

> Regrettably, the recent political experiences have been characterized by the corrupting influence of money on party politics and electioneering processes. This unwholesome practice has dire consequences on our nation, in subverting the exercise of free choice by voters, elevated corrupt and unprincipled individuals to positions of leadership and entrenching the structures of democracy devoid of accountability (Buhari, 2019b: 1).

Worse still, political parties in the Fourth Republic could be described as personal properties of godfathers, which they sell as a franchise to the highest bidder. This is a classic case of state capture by manipulating the electoral process to serve their individual and business interests. According to Akinduro and Masterson (2018: 68 - 69), these godfathers

> act as political entrepreneurs who are willing to 'sponsor' a candidate who will, in return, allow them to be the *de facto* decision makers for the office held by the beneficiary. The godfather and his businesses are also given preference in public procurement processes and in the nomination of persons to fill appointed positions in state organs (Akinduro and Masterson, 2018: 68–69).

It is in this context that we need to understand how those who, in the run-up to the 2019 General Elections, defected from one party to the other such as Senator Godswill Akpabio, who was made the "leader" of the APC in Akwa Ibom State[12]. Similarly, Senator Rabiu Kwankwaso was made the "leader" of the PDP in Kano State after he

---

[12] *Senator Akpabio was, until his defection to the APC in early August 2018, the Senate Minority Leader.*

decamped from the APC in July 2018. The structures of the party in the affected states were "handed over" to these leaders who assumed control over them. Also in Benue State, former Senate President, David Mark said on September 3, 2018 that he was handing over the PDP structures in the state to Governor Samuel Ortom who defected to the party from the APC in August 2018.

The point being made is that without any ideological orientation, Nigerian political parties are mere platforms for politicians to seek power for personal and other narrow interests. In these circumstances, criminal elements have become major actors in the political space. Narrow and personal interests become the dominant factors that inform public policy pursued by the predatory and rapacious elite. With this state of affairs, corruption thrives in Nigeria, and Nigerian politicians are generally seen to be corrupt. To quote Cardinal Onaiyekan (2018) again, "...the nation has been captured by corrupt people who have acquired massive power through the wealth they have stolen from us. They thus monopolize all channels of decision making."

Looting of the Commonwealth and the Competition for Corruption Medals by Politicians

Several elected officials have either been jailed or are facing various corruption charges. Those who have been convicted for corruption related offences include the ex-governor of Delta State, James Ibori (who was sentenced to 13 years in prison by a United Kingdom court); former governor of Taraba State, Jolly Nyame (sentenced to 14 years in prison); ex-governor of Adamawa State, James Ngilari (sentenced to five years in prison); ex-governor of Bayelsa State, the late Diepreye Alamieyeseigha (sentenced to two years); ex-governor of Plateau State, Joshua Dariye (sentenced to 14 years imprisonment), ex-governor of Edo State, Lucky Igbinedion and Orji Uzor Kalu former governor of Abia State, recently sentenced to 12 years in prison.

Nigeria: Democracy without Development. How to fix it

68

Other former ex-governors who have faced or are currently facing corruption charges are Ikedi Ohakim (Imo State); Jonah Jang (Plateau State); Attahiru Bafarawa (Sokoto State); Saminu Turaki (Jigawa State); Sule Lamido (Jigawa State); Isah Yuguda (Bauchi State); Adamu Mu'azu (Bauchi State); Chimaroke Nnamani (Enugu State); Senator Rasheed Ladoja (Oyo State); Boni Haruna (Adamawa State); Senator Bukola Saraki (Kwara State); Senator Ahmad Sani (Zamfara State); Senator Gabriel Suswam (Benue State); Martin Elechi (Ebonyi State); Senator Abdullahi Adamu (Nasarawa State); Gbenga Daniel (Ogun State); Senator George Akume (Benue State); Adebayo Alao-Akala (Oyo State); Ibrahim Shema (Katsina State); Mukhtar Ramalan Yero (Kaduna State); Peter Odili (Rivers); Danjuma Goje (Gombe); Abubukar Audu (Kogi State); Aliyu Akwe Doma (Nasarawa State); Timipre Sylva (Bayelsa State) and Ayodele Fayose (Ekiti State). This list seems to suggest that politicians are in competition to win a corruption medal!

Spouses of elected politicians are not left out of the looting of the national resources. Former First Lady, Dame Patience Jonathan, was on July 1, 2019 ordered by Justice Mojisola Olatoregun of the Federal High Court Lagos to forfeit $8.4 million and ₦9.2 billion to the Federal Government on the grounds that the funds were believed to be proceeds of crime.

The level of corruption in the country is anomalous and it has been one of the main factors for its poor development. As an illustration, according to the South-South Zonal Head of the Economic and Financial Crimes Commission (EFCC), Mr Naghe Obono-Itam, between 1999 and 2016, 80% of revenues meant for projects in the Niger Delta geo-political zone were diverted into private accounts. Consequently, developmental projects, including those for infrastructure, were not implemented.

He further amplified the depth of corruption in the country when he observed that, "80% of government revenues and budget allocations end up in the private bank accounts of approximately one percent of

Nigerians, who are linked to political power" (*Punch*, 2018c). As a consequence, "as high as 80 per cent of projects mentioned in annual state budgets within the region are either abandoned or never implemented" (*Punch*, 2018c).

And this is just a tip of the iceberg. In the estimation of the former governor of the Central Bank of Nigeria (CBN), Professor Charles Soludo, under the administration of President Goodluck Jonathan "probably more than ₦30 trillion has either been stolen or lost or unaccounted for or simply mismanaged ...in the past four years", 2010 – 2014 (Soludo, 2015). These examples show that not only are the political and administrative elite corrupt, they are also unable to manage the resources of the country for its development. In a talk at George Washington University, in Washington D.C., two-term Finance Minister, Dr Ngozi Okonjo-Iweala, attested to this when she acknowledged that in her second term as minister under President Jonathan, there was zero political will to save on behalf of the country. This was at a time when oil prices were at its highest.

Religion and Ethnic Divisiveness: Currencies of the Parasitic Political Elite

The Nigerian political elite promote and thrive on religion and ethnic divisiveness. They use them as political currency. In the period leading up to the 2019 General Elections, Nigerian social media was awash with news items that promoted religious and ethnic bigotry, as well as fake news. With a few exceptions, given the focus of the political class on narrow interests, they have little or no interest in transforming the Nigerian economy to move beyond its reliance on oil revenues. Furthermore, the political elite have not created social cohesion and a "Nigerian dream" that could be a rallying point for all Nigerians.

While most of the political class in the Fourth Republic profess to be members of the two dominant religions, Christianity and Islam, they

Nigeria: Democracy without Development. How to fix it

70

in fact worship what a Nigerian poet, Elnathan John (2012), refers to as the "Nigerian god"—a deity that lacks character, disdains hard work and righteousness, and whose primary preoccupation is the worship of money and corruption; who hates those of other faiths, as well as lacking respect for our common humanity and citizenship. Though written in a satirical manner, Elnathan John provides an apt description of the attitude of most Nigerian politicians:

> The Nigerian god loves elections and politics. When you have bribed people to get the Party nomination, used thugs to steal and stuff ballot boxes, intimidated people into either sitting at home or voting for you, lied about everything from your assets to your age, and you eventually, (through God's grace), win the elections, you must begin by declaring that your success is the wish of God and that the other candidate should accept this will of God. It is not your fault whom the Nigerian god chooses to reward with political success. How can mere mortals complain? (John, 2012).

In the end, their obsession with the "Nigerian god" has created a country that has lost its soul, moral compass and humanity. On Sundays, the churches are full, and on Fridays the mosques are full but daily, the halls of integrity are empty. Moral squalor pervades every street and corridor of power, and consequently defines governance. While Nigerians are some of the most religious people in the world, with about 95% of Nigerian Christians[13] praying daily (PEW, 2018), most Nigerians are ungodly since they do not follow the prescripts of the religion which they profess - hence the perverted valued system and the debasement of our common humanity. This perversion is carried over to governance – laws and rules are observed in the breach by a self-centred, myopic and unaccountable political class. It is therefore not by accident that the enhancement of human wellbeing is neglected in the democratic dispensation.

---

[13] *We can use this to generalise that about 95% Nigerian Muslims pray daily.*

71

Nigeria: Democracy without Development. How to fix it

In general, public affairs have been dominated by a parasitic and consuming elite whose *modus operandi* is transactional. With a few exceptions in business such as Aliko Dangote, who is now engaged in the real sector, the elite lack the vision and will to galvanise the productive capacity of the economy and society. It can safely be argued that most people that have presided over the political and economic affairs of Nigeria since independence have not been patriotic, and consequently were not developmental. Instead they have captured the Nigerian state for their selfish interests, and the situation has worsened since 1999. It is in the light of this that Cardinal Onaiyekan called on the political class to look after the wellbeing of Nigerians and not just their "fat salaries and allowances" (*Daily Trust*, 2018).

Neglect of the Health Sector and Nigeria as Cemetery of the Elite

The dominant elite in the Fourth Republic have not invested in the nation's health and education systems and have recklessly looted the commonwealth which they store in foreign countries. The elite have

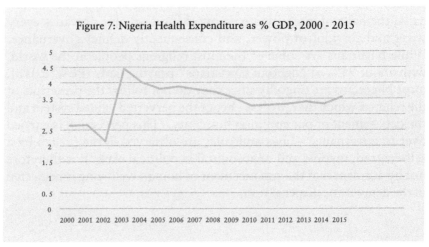

Figure 7: Nigeria Health Expenditure as % GDP, 2000 - 2015

Source: World Bank (2018d), WDI.

Nigeria: Democracy without Development. How to fix it

72

neglected investment in human capital development. As shown in
Figure 7, in 2014, in Africa's largest economy, Nigeria, healthcare
expenditure as a percentage of GDP was merely 2.64% in 2000 but
increased to only 3.56% in 2015.

In contrast, healthcare expenditure in Africa's second largest
economy, South Africa, increased from 7.44% in 2000 to 8.2% in
2015, as a percentage of GDP. The Nigerian health expenditure as a
percentage of GDP is lower than the sub-Saharan average of 5.38% in
2000 and 5.35% in 2015 (World Bank, 2018d). This is lower than
poorer African countries such as Swaziland and Malawi that
respectively spent 15.9% and 10.8% of government expenditure on
health in 2015 (World Health Organisation, 2018). The Nigerian
health system is consequently ranked among the lowest health systems
in the world.

Nigerian political office holders and civil servants transform overnight
into billionaires without owning factories or farms. The children of
the rich study overseas. Anecdotal evidence points to the fact that the
children of most ministers, governors, senators, members of the House
of Representatives, members of state assemblies, as well as other key
political appointees and senior civil servants study in universities
outside the country.

The poverty of the Nigerian political elite is further exemplified by the
poor physical infrastructure in the country as well as the high level of
insecurity. The country is descending into anarchy and has become a
killing field due to terrorism, robbery, kidnapping and banditry. On
top of all these, in Nigeria, people still die from preventable diseases.
The nation's healthcare system is so bad that the elite and their families
have to go for treatment abroad when they fall sick. Though life
expectancy at birth has increased from 47.19 years in 2000 to 53.8
years in 2017, Nigeria still has one of the lowest life expectancy rates
in the world. In 2017, it ranked 213 out of 224 countries
(IndexMundi, 2018a).

73

Nigeria: Democracy without Development. How to fix it

In general, one can argue that health institutions in the country remained mere consulting/prescription centres, thirty-seven years after then General Muhammadu Buhari used that as a justification for overthrowing President Shehu Shagari's administration in 1983. Ironically, beautiful fences enclosing dilapidated healthcare buildings with obsolete equipment and demotivated healthcare workers, who are at times unpaid for months, are the hallmarks of the Nigerian healthcare system. It is in this context that we need to understand that of the estimated 72,000 medical doctors who are registered with the Medical and Dental Council of Nigeria, only about 35,000 are currently practising in the country (see Banke-Thomas, n.d). Of these, over 25,000 and 6,000 Nigerian doctors are practicing in the United States of America and United Kingdom respectively. Leadership failure is thus one of the push factors of the high level of brain drain of medical professionals in the country.

Consequently, there is an acute shortage of medical doctors in the country. By 2010, Nigeria had 40 doctors to 1,000 people, which is below the World Health Organization (WHO) recommended doctor to population ratio of 1:1,000. The Nigerian ratio of doctors to population is lower than in South Africa (Africa's second largest economy) which is 77:1000, and also lower than Brazil, an emerging economy of 1.85:1.000 (IndexMundi, 2018b). By 2016, the situation had worsened. According to the data provided by the Medical and Dental Council of Nigeria (MDCN) to the *Premium Times*, the country had only 1 medical doctor for every 4,845 Nigerians. Again, this falls far below the WHO recommendation of 1 doctor to 600 patients for that year (*Premium Times,* 2019b).

Some of the deaths in Nigeria could have been prevented if there were good hospitals in the country to get immediate treatment once people fall ill. Former governor of Bayelsa State, Diepreye Alamieyeseigha, died a few hours before his planned evacuation for overseas treatment. His fate befalls thousands of Nigerians every year. To most of the elite, Nigeria is a cemetery where they are returned to be buried after they die in foreign hospitals. A number of key political leaders such as

Nigeria: Democracy without Development. How to fix it

74

former Vice President Alex Ekwueme died in foreign hospitals where they had gone to receive medical treatment. Similarly, former President Musa Yar' Adua returned virtually dead to the country from Saudi Arabia where he had gone for treatment, he died shortly after his return. Currently, former petroleum minister, Mrs Alison-Madueke, who allegedly stole millions of dollars and purchased choice properties within and outside the country, has been in London since 2015 for medical treatment. Even the incumbent president, Muhammadu Buhari has spent several months in London and elsewhere for medical treatment since he got into office four years ago. Buhari's wife, Aisha famously said that even the Aso Rock Clinic, for which millions of naira is allocated every year, could not produce a single syringe when she took ill in 2017. Buhari's son, Yusuf was flown abroad for treatment when he was involved in a motorcycle accident in 2018. These are just a few examples. Had the funds being taken abroad for such medical treatment been invested in the Nigerian health sector, all these people could have received treatment in Nigeria and such facilities would have served other Nigerians.

Politics of Rent-Seeking and Poor Governance

In the absence of a dominant Coalition of Developmentalists with a shared national vision and consensus, rent-seeking and its associated patronages have become the primary purpose of politics, and an emphasis of what divides rather than unites the nation and its people. It is in this context that we need to understand the resort to religion, ethnicity, state of origin, zoning, and the call for restructuring as defining characteristics of politics in the country.

It is not surprising that successive governments have made little contribution to Nigeria's economic, social and political development. It is clear that there is an absence of both a coalition of developmentalist elites and a broad DC with a common national vision and consensus about Nigeria's development and unity. As a result, every section of the Nigerian society feels marginalised. Regardless, the rent-seeking, retrogressive and consuming elite continue to have a field day looting the nation of its human and natural resources.

The absence of a coalition of developmentalist elites in the country has meant that a rapacious, consuming elite has presided over the affairs of the state for most of our independence period. They have and still poorly manage the country. One outcome of the poor management of the country is poor governance. Another is its dependence on crude oil, which the political elite is still unable to create the infrastructure to refine. They have also proved incapable of providing incentives for the generation and distribution of electricity to their citizens. The mismanagement of the economy by successive governments serves the interest of rent-seeking elites and *tenderpreneurs*—the latter depend mainly on government contracts. One major outcome of this is that the elite have not managed oil resources for a shared prosperity and to lay the foundation for a post-oil Nigerian economy. It is therefore not an accident that the economy has not been significantly diversified.

As shown in the previous chapter, Nigeria has a small and declining manufacturing sector. It is therefore not by accident that the economy went into recession in 2016 following the fall in global oil prices. It needs to be acknowledged that President Buhari is making efforts to diversify the economy, but this has remained minimal and the pace is too slow to have significant development impacts in the short to medium term.

Successive Nigerian administrations have mismanaged our oil wealth. Citizens are unable to take a regular supply of petrol for granted (Nigeria is the only oil producing country where citizens experience fuel scarcity). Similarly, they have not in any meaningful way, been able to create the conditions necessary to diversify the economy. Unfortunately, while this narrow production base (the formal sector) accounts for a substantial share of GDP, it has a low labour absorption rate and little downstream and upstream linkages to the rest of the

Nigeria: Democracy without Development. How to fix it

76

economy. It caters to the interests of a few people while the majority of Nigerians eke out a living in the non-formal and subsistence sectors. The Nigerian economy is therefore an enclave economy because the formal sector (oil and gas sector) has little positive development impact on the rest of the economy. This sector has imposed the resource curse on the country.

The high levels of poverty, inequality, unemployment and underemployment shown earlier, as well as stratospheric levels of corruption, are direct products of the absence of visionary and transformational leaders that are able to forge a developmentalist coalition that will transform the economy and invest in the country's most precious assets – the people of Nigeria, especially the youths. Evidence abounds that the Nigerian youth is considerably entrepreneurial and dynamic. In spite of this, the political leaders have not created an enabling environment for them to realise their full potentials. In effect, the political class has promoted an economic system that has denied the youths of social mobility. In the process, some of them have become merchants of crime and violence such as "419ners", "yahoo boys", kidnappers, terrorists, armed robbers and bandits.

The Nigerian situation is quite unlike other oil rich countries such as Norway. One factor that sets Norway apart from Nigeria is that in the former, there is a DC that foisted its vision of development, namely social democracy, on the state and society. Because of this orientation, successive Norwegian governments since the discovery of oil in 1969 have ensured that they manage their oil wealth to cater for the wellbeing of present and future generations of their people (Norway is consequently ranked first on all major human development indicators). Norwegian political leaders do not pillage the country's wealth; rather, they save and invest massively in their people, including the provision of free education and healthcare for all citizens.

77

Nigeria: Democracy without Development. How to fix it

Norway's Sovereign Wealth Fund is estimated at one trillion United States Dollars ($1,000,000,000). This translates to the fact that each of the five million Norwegians would receive $200,000 if savings from its oil was divided among its citizens. Furthermore, the elite in Norway have used rent from oil to diversify their economy. This has been possible because, as Jonathon Moses (2010) argued in his insightful work on the management of Norwegian oil wealth, the Norwegian elite built robust and inclusive state institutions for efficient management of oil wealth – and as a basis to diversify the country's economy.

In Nigeria, the problem *per say* is not the absence of developmentalist oriented individuals in the country. Such individuals can be found in all segments of the Nigerian society - in government (in elective positions and the bureaucracy), the private sector, the media, the academia, in communities, civil society organisations and political parties. The problem is the absence of a coalition for these patriotic elites to forge a broad developmentalist alliance with social groups that share their vision of development. As a consequence, they are unable to act in a collective and cohesive manner to prioritise investments in Nigeria's greatest asset – its people – and to transform the structure of the economy.

Lack of Comprehensive Development Vision and the Problem of Abandoned Projects

Developmentalists in the country have hardly made any significant contribution to change the course of Nigerian development partly because of the non-existence of informal and formal platforms to regularly interact, share ideas and garner support in their various professional callings, as well as to coordinate activities among themselves. The few developmentalists in positions of authority have been confronted with numerous challenges which make them unable to sustain institutional and policy reforms. Also, in the absence of an

Nigeria: Democracy without Development. How to fix it

78

informal platform for mutual support and reinforcement, those of them in authority are consumed by rent-seeking and pervasive corruption in the political system, while others have been frustrated and capitulated. Developmentalists who manage to bring about some positive developmental changes when in leadership positions have seen such gains reversed by their successors. The frequent policy somersaults in Nigeria and the non-institutionalisation of reforms are partly the consequences of the absence of a DC. This is evidenced in the area of articulating a National Development Vision (NDV).

Since 1999, the political class has not articulated an NDV that has been consistently implemented. Successive administrations have articulated different NDVs which were abandoned by their successors: Vision 20:2020 (President Obasanjo), Seven Point Agenda (President Yar' ardua), Transformation Agenda (President Jonathan) and Economic Recovery and Growth Plan (President Buhari). Another example of policy somersault is in the power sector reform. The administration of President Olusegun Obasanjo adopted a policy to privatise the power sector. In contrast, the administration of his hand-picked successor from the same party, President Umaru Yar' ardua, suspended the privatisation exercise. This was reversed by President Jonathan, who implemented the privatisation of the sector with vigour.

This attitude is extended to projects whereby those initiated by one administration are abandoned by their successors, thus entrenching the phenomenon of abandoned projects in the country. To illustrate this point, the report of the Presidential Projects Assessment Committee (PPAC) set up by the former president, Goodluck Jonathan, looked into cases of abandoned projects. The report showed that there were 11,886 abandoned projects in the country, with an estimated cost of ₦7.78 trillion needed to complete them. A subsequent survey in 2017 by the Chartered Institute of Project Management (CIMP) of Nigeria, showed that abandoned projects in the country were estimated to cost the nation ₦12 trillion (*The Sun*, 2017).

79

Nigeria: Democracy without Development. How to fix it

The abandonment of development projects has profound adverse effects on the country and its people. These include "disappointment of the populace/users, low living standards, wastage of resources, reduction in employment opportunities, decrease in tempo of construction activities, decrease in revenue accruing to government, difficulty in attracting foreign loans *and investments, as well as endangered the ease of doing business in the country*" (Ayodele, 2011: 142, *emphasis added*).

The phenomenon of abandoned projects has slowed the pace of Nigeria's development and has resulted in an infrastructural deficit which is estimated at between ₦12 trillion and ₦17 trillion naira. In turn, the country's low industrial base and low manufacturing capacities are due to the poor state of its infrastructure. At the heart of this problem of abandoned projects is corruption as public officials want to initiate new projects to receive commissions or bribes. In addition, unscrupulous contractors abandon projects for which they have been paid in part or in full, and because there are no consequences, these contractors have generally gotten away with it. Abandonment of projects is just another means of looting the Nigerian commonwealth.

It should be noted that the administration of President Buhari is trying to reverse this trend by working vigorously to complete capital projects initiated by his predecessors. However, the problem of not articulating and consistently implementing long-term development visions will continue unless developmentalist elites, for their own enlightened self-interest, come together to forge a common vision and take practical steps to realise it. The poor leadership in all sectors in the country partly reflects the absence of a DC that can foist a productivist, ethical and patriotic ethos as the defining values of Nigeria.

As noted earlier, one product of this is that since 1999, the country has been marked by politics bereft of ideology, resulting in random cross-carpeting by politicians for personal financial gain and power for its

Nigeria: Democracy without Development. How to fix it

80

own sake rather than in pursuit of a tangible national goal. The ultimate outcome of this is the systematic looting of the commonwealth with impunity by the political class and their collaborators in the private sector. The poor quality of political leadership in Nigeria since the advent of liberal democracy has ultimately resulted in the economic non-inclusivity shown in Chapter Two.

Insecurity and the Political Elite as Conflict Entrepreneurs

The political elite thrive on divisions. As a result, ethno-religious conflicts have been exacerbated in the democratic dispensation due to the activities of some in the political class who have become conflict entrepreneurs. A number of ethnic militia and terrorist groups have also emerged. Hundreds of innocent people have been killed in these conflicts. According to the International Crisis Group (2018), 1500 people were killed since September 2017, of these, 1300 were killed in the first half of 2018 alone in Nigeria.

The most recent of these conflicts is the cattle herders and farmers violence, which some argue is perpetuated by nomadic Fulani herdsmen against largely Christian farmers. A closer examination however, reveals that these conflicts are driven by economic interests rather than religious and ethnic interests. As the International Crisis Group (2018) rightly observed, "The conflict is fundamentally a land-use contest between farmers and herders across the country's Middle Belt". One of Nigeria's leading public intellectuals, Jibrin Ibrahim (2019) identified several factors that have led to the rise in the herdsmen-farmers crisis. These include the following:

> The first was the collapse of local government and the end (sic)
> public administration of the traditional burti system of cattle
> routes (burtali) that ensured that the cattle could move
> without destroying crops by encroaching on farms. The

81

Nigeria: Democracy without Development. How to fix it

second was the explosion of Fadama agriculture following the success of the World Bank agriculture development projects. With high value agriculture around the sources of dry season water, cattle could no longer access the water and grass in the Fadama and had to move elsewhere. The third factor was medical – effective treatment of trypanosomes and other diseases that had made cattle rearing in more humid environments in the South previously impossible without significant losses to the herds. Medical advances meant the herds could move to the forest zone without significant loss. Communal conflicts arise when grazing cattle are not properly controlled and consequently graze on cultivated plants like cassava, maize, etc.

Another factor for the herders-farmers conflict is what he termed as the absence of the state in rural areas, in terms of providing social protections and security. But while the state is unable to provide basic infrastructure and services to rural communities, it is present in these communities through weak and corrupt judicial officials as well as corrupt law enforcement officials that mete punitive measures on rural communities, including farmers and herders. According to Ibrahim, this absence of justice where there are conflicts between herdsmen and farmers exacerbates the crisis between the two groups.

What this analysis points to is that the herders-farmers conflict is primarily due to contests over economic resources and to poor governance, rather than religion and ethnicity. Criminal elements have taken advantage of these conflicts to unleash terror in both Muslim and Christian communities. Villages and schools have been destroyed, thousands of people, including school pupils have been displaced. Again, the research of the International Crisis Group showed that:

> The conflict's roots lie in climate-induced degradation of pasture and increasing violence in the country's far north, which have forced herders south; the expansion of farms and

Nigeria: Democracy without Development. How to fix it

82

settlements that swallow up grazing reserves and block traditional migration routes; and the damage to farmers' crops wrought by herders' indiscriminate grazing (International Crisis Group, 2018).

This crisis is evidenced in the North West geo-political zone, including Kaduna State. Banditry has become widespread in the country. By July 2018, the crisis had spread to Zamfara State, a predominantly Muslim State, where bandits have killed hundreds of innocent people. Images of people fleeing from their communities are awash in social media. Kidnapping is also rampant and generally, Nigeria has become a killing field.

The problem is that the Nigerian state and the political class lack the political will and political capacity to address these conflicts and insecurity in the country. Many politicians try to gain political capital by playing one religion or ethnic group against the other. In 2018, Nigeria was ranked the 22nd most unsafe country out of 117 countries in the world (Numbeo, 2018). The insecurity in the country has denied citizens "freedom from fears", which in turn erodes the legitimacy and credibility of democracy in the country. As Afrobarometer shows, like in most African countries, the Nigerian people are ready to trade freedom – a key pillar of democracy – for security (Logan and Penar, 2019). It should be noted that a state that cannot protect its people cannot be said to be democratic. In a democracy, freedom reigns.

In the absence of a developmentalist ideology, there is a general distrust of Nigerian politicians by citizens. The World Economic Forum Global Competitiveness Index (2017) shows that Nigeria is one of the countries where citizens have the least trust in their politicians. On a scale of 1 to 7, where 7 is highest trust of politicians, and 1 is least trust, Nigeria scored 1.59 in 2017. In general, between 2008 and 2012, citizen trust in Nigerian politicians rose from 1.48 to 2.23. Since then, citizens have consistently lost trust in their politicians. By 2017, trust in Nigerian politicians had declined to 1.59 (World Bank, 2017).

In fact, ordinary citizens do not trust their government at any level. The trust deficits of Nigerian politicians erode the legitimacy of democracy. As the data by Afrobarometer shows, there has been declining citizen satisfaction with democracy. By 2014, only 24% of Nigerians were satisfied with democracy in the country. This was one of the lowest levels of satisfaction among 28 countries in sub-Saharan Africa assessed by Afrobarometer.

In the context of poverty, some citizens demand their "democracy dividends" in the form of being paid before they vote, which as noted earlier makes some citizens see the election cycle as harvest time. This has entrenched the culture of vote-buying in the Nigerian political system. In fact, Nigeria's democracy can be aptly described as *cash and carry*.

Conclusion: Mal-Governance in Nigeria

In general, democracy in Nigeria in the twenty-first century can be described as what I referred to elsewhere as mal-governance. It is "marked by exclusion of the people from governance, non-accountability of public officials, lack of transparency and the colonialisation and personalisation of the state and national resources by the political elite" (Edigheji, 2005: 2). In addition, it is unable to address the demands and respond to the needs of a majority of the Nigerian people. Consequently, Nigeria cannot be labelled a democracy. This conclusion is supported even from a narrow conception of democracy.

In its Democracy Index, the Economic Intelligence Unit (EIU) (2019) grouped countries into four regime types, namely: full democracies, flawed democracies, hybrid regimes and authoritarian regimes. It classified Nigeria as a hybrid democracy between 2015 and 2018. As a hybrid regime, the country combined features of democracy with that of authoritarianism. As the analysis in this chapter shows, while

Nigeria: Democracy without Development. How to fix it

84

Nigeria holds regular elections, they are marked by fraudulent processes that prevent citizens from freely choosing their political leaders. At the same time, repression of political opponents, low political participation and violation of civil liberties are commonplace. Consequently, the EIU ranked Nigeria 108 out of 167 countries in its democracy index. The next chapter sets out the institutional architecture that underpins the poor development performance of electoralism in the country.

85

Nigeria: Democracy without Development. How to fix it

Chapter Four

The Institutional Deficits of Nigerian Democracy

Introduction

Having regular multi-party elections is one thing; building institutions that drive development is another. In this chapter it will be shown that while the governance indicators that constitute the focus of electoral democracy matter and are necessary, they are not sufficient conditions to drive a developmentalist agenda. History and theory support this proposition. As a result, this chapter begins by highlighting the limitations of these indicators.

Seeing Like the Market: Institutions in the Good Governance Paradigm

The good governance paradigm became the mantra of democracy in the 1990s with international development agencies such as the United Nations Development Programme (UNDP), the World Bank and bilateral agencies, as its main proponents in Africa. Components of the good governance trumpeted by these agencies included regular multi-party elections, the rule of law, transparency, accountability, decentralisation and citizen participation.

As noted by Rita Abrahamsen (2000), this agenda focused on superficial democratic institutional forms that are compatible with the neo-liberal agenda. In a similar vein, Murisa argues that the "democracy is equal to elections" mantra, has "varying consequences for governance, economic development and the manner in which political power is exercised. In many ways, it has led to an elite-based and unaccountable dynastic form of politics strengthened by clientelist relations that fuel corruption and entrench inequality" (Murisa, 2015b). The analysis in this book supports this proposition.

Key thinkers of governance in the World Bank like Daniel Kaufmann, Aart Kraay and Massimo Mastruzzi (2009) developed a dataset on six governance indicators, covering the period between 1996 to 2002. These indicators are clustered around three areas, namely (1) the process by which governments are selected, monitored and replaced; (2) the capacity of the government to effectively formulate and implement sound policies; and (3) the respect of citizens and the state for the institutions that govern interactions.

These indicators, like other indicators from international development agencies, have a number of commonalities. They focus on the nature of the political regime, the process of selecting leaders, civil and political liberties and the rule of law. However, one utility of the Kaufmann *et al.* dataset is that it includes indicators on state

Nigeria: Democracy without Development. How to fix it

88

capacity. Indeed, there are a host of international organisations that are primarily trying to develop data on state institutions. These include Freedom House and Polity, but from such narrow conceptual frames of democracy—their primary focus is on civil and political liberties. While they might be important, they are barking up the wrong tree. This is because, as stated previously, while voting and indeed elections matter, they are not enough in terms of shaping policies and their outcomes.

Governments, whether democratic or non-democratic have, on some occasions, produced the same or similar outcomes. In other words, the nature of electoral regimes is not the main factor for shaping or determining policy outcomes. Hence there are democratic countries, such as the Nordic countries that have achieved successful development performance and there are the East Asian developmental states, which though were initially not democratic but recorded remarkable socio-economic progress for more than four decades, and have remained the fastest growing economies in the world.

In light of the above, rather than focus exclusively on the nature of the political regime and the manner in which political office holders are elected, we should broaden our enquiries to the administrative structures of the state. Specifically, there is a need to focus on how the public sector is organised, how civil servants are recruited, their incentive structures, the coordination of government's socio-economic activities and policies, as well as the nature of the interactions between the government and socio-economic actors. These are the factors that shape policies and policy outcomes.

Similarly, trade-offs around competing social and economic policies and priorities by interest groups are made in institutional settings of the state, and between the state and societal actors. Differences in such key indicators explain variations in development performance. Empirical studies by a number of scholars have shown this (Evans and Rauch, 1999; Edigheji, 2007 and Kohli, 2010). Therefore, focusing on such institutional attributes that drive developmentalism should be the focus in a discussion of democracy across the globe, including Nigeria.

The work of Kaufmann *et al.* has an immediate appeal because of its reference to "government effectiveness" and "institutions that govern the interactions between the state and society". On closer examination however, institutions in this case are defined in the tradition of Ostrom (1986) and North (1990), as rules and legal norms. This tradition defines institutions as rules that govern and constrain the actions of actors. Hence the emphasis is on the rule of law and enforceability of contracts. However, the Nigerian experience, like the rest of the African continent, has shown that the observance of the rule of law and enforceability of contracts are not sufficient conditions to transform the structure of the economy, or improve the living conditions of a majority of its people.

This book highlights the need to focus on the organisational structures of the state and the consultative mechanisms between the state and societal actors if Nigerian democracy is to be developmental. Organisational arrangements of the state and those that govern and structure its interactions with non-state actors are the arenas for shaping and determining policies and their outcomes (Edigheji, 2007).

Even when the Kaufmann *et al.*'s dataset includes bureaucratic quality as one of the defining variables of "government effectiveness" and a proxy for institutional structure, it does not define the shape or determine the quality of the bureaucracy. However, as work on the developmental state has shown, it is Weberianess — that is meritocratic recruitment and well-defined career paths for civil servants (thus a professional and career civil service) — that determines the effectiveness of a bureaucracy. Also of importance is the presence of a coordinating ministry that occupies a central place in shaping economic policy. These are powerful explanatory variables and/or determinants of the quality of the bureaucracy. In effect, bureaucratic quality in particular and state capacity in general is derived from the Weberianess of the state and its planning capacity. Therefore, the debate on democracy and development (democratic development) in Nigeria must be situated within this institutional context—institutions as organisations/structures, as Evans (1995) and others have done in the case of the developmental state of Asia.

Kaufmann *et al.*'s contribution has another important value: it includes an indicator to measure "the capacity of the government to effectively formulate and implement sound policies" (Kaufmann et al., 2009: 2), which they called government effectiveness. They aggregated several indices to constitute this variable, namely, "the quality of public service provision, the quality of the bureaucracy, the competence of civil servants, the independence of civil servants from political pressures, and the credibility of government's commitment to policies" (p3). This definition of state capacity is however, flawed because some of these indices are outcomes. Therefore, contrary to their assertion, they equate outcomes with inputs. To draw on Michael Mann (2003), this is to substitute the institutionality of the state – internal institutional attributes – with its functionality, that is, its functions (Edigheji, 2007).

The fundamental question is, why are some states more effective than others? The answer lies in the institutional characteristics of the state, which in turn determines its effectiveness/capacity. A closer look at the indices that constitute the government effectiveness indicator by Kaufmann *et al.* show that they are outcomes that are derivable from both the nature and character of economic state institutions, especially state autonomy. Some of the indices include the quality of the bureaucracy/institutional effectiveness, excessive bureaucracy/red tape, the administrative and technical skills of top civil servants, the state's ability to formulate and implement national policy initiatives, the ability to coordinate policy within the central bureaucracy and between the national and other levels of government. They also include the ability to monitor socio-economic trends, the ability to respond effectively to domestic problems, the ability of the state to carry out its declared programmes and government economic policies, and being independent of pressure from special interests.

91

Nigeria: Democracy without Development. How to fix it

All of the issues enumerated above are dependent on the institutional infrastructure of the state. Though the authors correctly defined the indicator as state capacity, it should not be equated with the "sources" of state capacity. In fact, such indices are not sources of state capacity but its products. They therefore help to explain the capacity of the state and its behaviour rather than the source(s) of such capacity. Consequently, the indices used to compose the indicators are dependent on the institutional composition and character of the state. These include meritocratic recruitment and career paths for economic technocrats who are concentrated in core economic planning agencies/ministries. These are where the sources of state capacity, which Michael Mann (2003) calls infrastructural power, is derived. This is what enables the state to coordinate its activities and forge cooperative relationships with key societal economic actors in order to achieve its developmental goals, especially in a democratic setting.

Another attempt at developing indicators for state capacity, or more narrowly, bureaucratic capacity, is The International Civil Service Effectiveness (InCiSE) Index by the Blavatnik School of Government and the Institute for Government, Oxford University (2017). This is one of the few attempts by scholars to develop indices to measure civil service effectiveness. They came up with six attributes to measure state effectiveness, namely: integrity, openness, capabilities, inclusiveness, staff engagement and innovation. A closer examination of these indexes shows that they have mixed explanatory variables with outcomes, (dependent variables). For instance, besides openness, which they define as "regular practice and degree of the civil service engagement with citizens", the attributes/indexes are dependent variables. However, the capabilities index defined as "the extent of which the civil service workforce has the right mix of skills" is surely an outcome of ensuring that there is meritocracy in recruitment into the service.

In light of these, the InCiSE index is not the most effective tool to measure state capacity in general and bureaucratic effectiveness in particular. This leaves us with variables in the developmental state

Nigeria: Democracy without Development. How to fix it

92

literature, that is, "embedded autonomy" as the most effective tools to explain sources of state capacity. Hence, this book is framed within this literature. We will return to this later in our discussion of the Nigerian state.

Politics of Presence: The Marginalisation of Women in Nigerian

The discussion of electoral democracy in Nigeria, as in other parts of the continent, perhaps with the exception of Rwanda and South Africa, has largely ignored the question of *politics of presence or symbolic representation*. Nigerian politics has largely been driven by primordial factors such as religion and ethnicity. Territorial representation is the dominant trend in the country. Symbolic representation or politics of presence is only practiced in its crudest forms, with focus on ethnicity and religion. It is generally accepted that the President and the Vice President of Nigeria cannot come from the same region or religion—and that the North and the South produce the president in rotation. Thus if a presidential candidate is a Muslim from the North, the running mate must be a Christian from the South, and when a northerner completes his/her term, a southerner will replace him/her. This has been the trend since independence. The one exception was in 1993 when the Abiola-Kingibe ticket was a Muslim-Muslim ticket. In the Fourth Republic (since 1999), the North-South and Christian-Muslim balances have been maintained. However, a symbolic representation of other identities such as gender, disabilities and age are firmly ignored.

The argument in favour of politics of presence is that representatives from previously marginalised groups are more aware, more sensitive and better suited to represent the interests of their members/constituents than those outside the group. As Zappala (1999, cited in Edigheji, 2006) has argued in the case of gender:

> ...several studies suggest that gender does influence both representatives and their constituents' attitudes to

representation, from style of doing politics to having greater empathy for policies that assist a better balance to work and female. Female parliamentarians are also more responsive to issues of concern to women constituents.

This has largely been ignored in Nigeria. Consequently, men have dominated Nigerian politics. As shown in Table 2 below, since 1999, all four presidents and four vice presidents have been male. At the ministerial level, 85.06% of the 241 ministers have been male. In July 2019, President Buhari announced the nomination of 43 ministers for his second term. Out of these, only seven, that is 16%, were women. Also, as can be seen in Table 2, in the four administrations since May 1999 to May 2019, 93.81% of senators have been male compared to 6.19% female. Also, all the principal officers of the senate, including the Senate President and Deputy Senate President, have been male. Out of the 1440 members of the House of Representatives in the period from May 1999 to May 2019, only 93 members, that is 6.46%, have been female, compared to 1,347 (93.54%) male. The only female to have emerged as Speaker of the House in July 2007, Patricia Ette, was removed after barely five months in office. The declining trend of women representation continued in the 9th National Assembly that was inaugurated on June 11, 2019. Out of 101 Senators, only 7 were women, while of the 360 Members of House of Representatives sworn in, only 11 were women.

The situation is not different at the sub-national level. All the 154 governors in the period between May 1999 and May 2019 in the Fourth Republic were males. In the same vein, 87.2% of 164 deputy governors have been male compared to 12.8% (21) female. Out of the 2850 members of state house of assemblies since 1999, only 168 (5.89%) have been female compared to 2682 (94.11%) male. Again, like in previous elections, there was no woman among the 29 governors that were elected in the 2019 General Elections. Only three female deputy governors were elected, namely, Ezeilo Cecilia Ibioma (Enugu State), Dr Hadiza Sabuwa Balarabe (Kaduna State) and Noimot Salako-Oyedele (Ogun State).

What these figures show is that democracy has not been inclusive – women are excluded from elective and other leadership positions. The same is true of the youths. It can therefore be argued that Nigerian democracy is exclusionary, leaving out women and youths. An electoral process that makes it impossible for women and youths to be elected is not a democracy.

The report of the European Union Observer Mission (EOM) to the 2019 General Elections highlighted some of the factors that account for the low representation of women in politics. These include "lack of legal requirements for the promotion of women in political life. Parties continue to lack policies and practices to promote women in party leadership or as candidates" (EOM, 2019: 48). Other factors include the dominance of money in politics, women cannot afford the prohibitive cost to run for elective office; political violence, gender-based intimidation and sexual harassment; the nocturnal nature of politics (meetings are held at odd hours) and; a patriarchal (and even religious) culture that views women's role as homemakers and discourages their participation in politics. It is not uncommon to hear people refer to women in politics as *ashawo*, that is, prostitutes. Consequently, as the EOM report points out, Nigeria has the lowest rate of women parliamentarians in Africa and has failed to meet the 35% national target of women in elected positions prescribed in the National Gender Policy of 2006.

95

Nigeria: Democracy without Development. How to fix it

Table 2: Political Representation by Gender

Male Ministerial Political Positions					
	2003	2007	2011	2015	Total
Male	38	83	53	31	205 (85.06%)
Female	4	12	15	5	36 (14.94%)
Total	42	95	68	36	241

Male Governor and Deputy Governors					
	2003	2007	2011	2015	Total
Governor (M)	37	40	41	36	154 (100%)
Governor (F)	0	0	0	0	0
Dep. Governor (M)	36	35	39	33	143 (87.20)
Dep. Governor (F)	3	4	8	6	21 (12.80)
Dep. Governor (T)	39	39	47	39	164

Male Representatives in National Parliament					
	2003	2007	2011	2015	Total
Senate (M)	106	100	102	101	409 (93.81%)
Senate (F)	3	9	7	8	27 (6.19%)
Senate (T)	109	109	109	109	436
House of Rep (M)	339	335	336	337	1,347 (93.54%)
House of Rep (F)	21	25	24	23	93 (6.46%)
House of Rep (T)	360	360	360	360	1440

keys: (M) - Male, (F) - Female, (T) - Total

Nigeria: Democracy without Development. How to fix it

96

Male Principal Officers at the Senate by Office[14]

	2003	2007	2011	2015	Total
Senate President (M)	2	1	1	1	5
Senate President (F)	0	0	0	0	0
Dep Senate President	1	1	1	1	
Majority Leader	1	1	1	1	
Dep Majority Leader	1	1	1	1	
Minority Leader	1	1	1	1	
Dep Minority Leader	1	1	1	1	
Chief Whip	2	1	1	1	
Dep Chief Whip	2	1	1	1	
Minority Whip	2	1	1	1	
Dep Minority Whip	1	1	1	0	

Members of States' House of Assemblies

	2003	2007	2011	2015	Total
Legislator (M)	710	663	650	659	2682 (94.11%)
Legislators (F)	30	43	58	37	168 (5.89%)
Total	740	706	708	696	2850

Male Principal Officers in State Assemblies by Gender

	2003	2007	2011	2015
Speaker (M)	49	51	74	44
Speakers (F)	2	1	2	3
Deputy Speaker (M)	45	47	44	41
Deputy Speakers (F)	1	3	1	2

House Maj Leaders (M)	47	43	43	40
House Maj Leaders (F)	1	1	1	0
Dep House Maj Leader (M)	31	31	33	40
Dep House Maj Leaders (F)	2	1	2	1
House Min Leaders (M)	27	21	28	29
House Min Leaders (F)	1	2	2	3
Dep House Min Leaders (M)	20	19	17	20
Dep House Min Leaders (F)	0	0	0	0
House Chief Whips (M)	35	39	36	52
House Chief Whips (F)	1	2	7	2
Dep House Chief Whip (M)	26	23	24	26
Dep House Chief Whips (F)	2	6	4	4
House Min Whips (M)	18	15	17	20
House Min Whips (F)	1	2	7	2
Dep House Min Whip (M)	68	68	68	73
Dep House Min Whips (F)	3	1	1	0
Committee ChairPerson (M)	492	557	549	574
Committee ChairPersons (F)	50	38	50	33

Source: National Council of Women and Development

It is clear from the above that women have been marginalised in political participation. Therefore, Nigerian politics is not inclusive and does not accommodate diversity. The marginalisation of women is also evidenced in the civil service, especially at the higher levels. There have been more male than female civil servants, especially at management levels such as the permanent secretary cadre. This is a factor that has often been ignored. As a consequence, the needs of women are not incorporated into public policy. It is therefore not surprising that the development outcomes since 1999 have been unfavourable to women.

Nigeria: Democracy without Development. How to fix it

98

Marginalisation of the Youth in Nigerian Politics

Like women, the Nigerian youths are another important group that are marginalised in the political space. This is in spite of the fact that they constitute a significant number of the population and of voters. Of about 200 million Nigerians, those between the ages of 18 and 30 years are estimated to be around 33.7 million and of the 84 million registered voters for the 2019 General Elections, those below the age of thirty years constituted 51%, yet the political class has excluded them from mainstream politics in the last two decades of democracy. They are under represented as candidates for elective offices. For example, only 0.1% of candidates presented in the 25 state houses of assembly in the 2019 elections were under the age of 30 (EOM, 2019). Since 1999, there has not been any minister under the age of 30 years.

It seems that politicians have confined the role of the youths in the electoral process to political thuggery, especially during party primaries and general elections. In the latter, people are regularly maimed and killed by political thugs. When closely examined, one finds that the perpetrators are young people working on behalf of politicians, who pay them peanuts during elections and abandon them in post-election period. In the post-election period, some politicians even maintain a coterie of thugs that they use to harass both opponents and perceived opponents. Some of these political thugs, armed by politicians, turn to full time criminality including armed robbery, kidnapping, banditry and terrorism. This partly accounts for the high level of insecurity in the country since 1999, which has consistently been on the rise.

State Capacity for Development: Autonomy – Weak and Dysfunctional Nigerian Bureaucracy

In analysing the governance architecture that must drive developmentalism in Nigeria, there is a need to focus on the state institutional administrative structures, its ideological orientation (especially technical, administrative and political capacities that underpin its planning, coordination and implementation capacities) and the institutional forms of engagement with citizens and non-state actors in the development process.[15] This brings to the fore the work on democratic developmental states.

As noted above, in the dominant "good governance" framework, the focus is more on "governance" as a process rather than the substantive outcomes of development. It emphasises issues of representative democracy, rule of law, decentralisation, transparency, accountability, and human rights. This framework does not give much attention to development outcomes and the competent, professional and career-oriented bureaucracy that should underpin development governance as well as the nature and character of a political class that should drive developmentalism.

This is partly because Nigeria's democracy is predicated on a neo-liberal agenda[16] that limits the role of the state to that of a night watchman and the pursuit of austerity measures which is inimical to structural transformation and an inclusive economy. More than twenty years after African scholars and policymakers demonstrated the adverse effects of SAPs on development, three economists of the IMF, Jonathan D. Ostry, Prakash Loungani, and Davide Furceri have come to the same conclusion in a recently published paper titled "Neoliberalism: Oversold?" They observed that:

> Openness and austerity are associated with increasing income inequality; this distributional effect sets up an adverse feedback loop. The increase in inequality engendered by financial openness and austerity might itself undercut growth, the very thing that the neoliberal agenda is intent on boosting. There is now strong evidence that inequality can significantly

---

15   *This book will be limited to the autonomy variable. That is, it will not deal with deliberative democracy.*
16   *This Washington Consensus and its good governance framework were made conditions by the World Bank and IMF for their engagement with Africa and other developing countries, especially those in Latin America. Western bilateral donors also bought into this agenda.*

lower both the level and the durability of growth (Ostry et al., 2016:41).

They went further to observe that

> in practice, episodes of fiscal consolidation have been followed, on average, by drops rather than by expansions in output. On average, a consolidation of 1 percent of GDP increases the long-term unemployment rate by 0.6 percentage point and raises by 1.5 percent within five years the Gini measure of income inequality (Ostry et al., 2016:40)

In summary, they concluded that some of the perceived benefits of the neo-liberal agenda are exaggerated.

An interesting point to note is that the IMF reached this conclusion only when developed countries were being required to adopt austerity packages. The cry of progressive African scholars and some policymakers about the adverse effects of such policy measures were ignored by the Bretton Woods institutions and developed countries. Instead, African countries were forced to swallow the bitter pills that were SAPs. To be sure, African scholars and policymakers have continued to stress the importance of growth that has positive impact on the lives of the people of the continent.

The current president of the African Development Bank (AfDB), Akinwumi Adesina, has used every opportunity to press home this point. In a tweet on January 25, 2018, he poignantly observed that "GDP growth is not enough. Growth must be felt in lives of people. Nobody eats GDP" (Adesina, 2018). He correctly underlined the point that growth must impact on people's lives by reducing poverty and increasing employment. This is a real paradigm shift for the AfDB because, for decades, it parroted and promoted the Washington Consensus on the continent.

The adoption of a neo-liberal economic agenda was encompassing in its effects, including the retrenchment of the state. It entailed privatisation, outsourcing, downsizing and rightsizing of the state, public-private-partnerships, commodification, and so on. All of these resulted in a lean state with a reliance on the market seen by the Bretton Woods institutions as the most efficient allocator of resources. The adoption of the neo-liberal framework has contributed to an increase in poverty, inequality and unemployment. Crucially, it did not lead to income growth. Foreign Direct Investment (FDI) that was parroted as one of its most likely benefits was elusive. As a consequence, the 1980s and 1990s, during which the military regime led by General Ibrahim Babangida imposed what he termed home-grown SAPs on the country, have been dubbed "Nigeria's Lost Decades".

To a large extent, Nigeria is a choiceless democracy: it mainstreamed its development agendas within global development frameworks such as the World Bank-inspired Poverty Reduction Strategies (PRSPs); the Millennium Development Goals (MDGs) Global Goals that are promoted by the United Nations, and the good governance framework promoted by both the UNDP and the World Bank. These frameworks are predominantly predicated on neo-liberalism. They entail privatisation, rightsizing the state, outsourcing of key government functions to the private sector, and so on. These are coupled with the process of *agentification*, meaning the fragmentation of state institutions by establishing executive agencies to undertake specific roles or functions considered to be non-core to the public service. They are pursued under the New Public Management (NPM) paradigm that informed the country's public sector reforms and with the resultant incapacitation of the Nigerian state. The irony is that these reforms that reduced the role of the state in the development process were carried out in the name of democratic governance.

The socio-economic reforms and agenda that was predicated on the dominant global market fundamentalism not only hampered the capacity of the state to affect structural reforms to industrialise, but also to substantively improve the livelihood of Nigerians. The country witnessed de-industrialisation beginning in the 1980s as many industries were closed and workers lost their jobs. History has shown that democracies that aggressively hamper the capacity of the state to promote the structural transformation of the economy and social justice cannot engender inclusive growth. In recognition of this, the United Nations Conference on Trade and Development (UNCTAD) produced a report in 2009, entitled *The State and Development Governance*. It coined the term "good development governance" or "governance for development" that focused on the process, institutions and outcomes of governance. It argues that good development governance:

> is about creating a better future for members of a society through using the authority of the state to promote economic development, and in particular to catalyse structural transformation...Development governance is oriented to solve common national development problems, create new national development opportunities and achieve common national goals. This is simply not a matter of designing appropriate institutions, but also a question of policies and the processes through which they are formulated and implemented. Which institutions matter is inseparable from which policies are adopted. Development governance is thus about the processes, policies and institutions associated with purposefully promoting national development and ensuring a socially legitimate and inclusive distribution of its costs and benefits (UNCTAD, 2009: VI).

Therefore, for democracy to engender developmentalism, the state needs to play an active role. In the Nigerian context, this calls for a democratic developmental state, a subject that has been a preoccupation of some African scholars for about two decades(Mkandawire, 1995; Edigheji, 2005 and 2010; and Olukoshi, 2011), as well as development agencies such as the United Nations Economic Commission for Africa (ECA, 2011). The APRM's African

Charter on Democracy, Elections and Governance re-echoed this call for a new form of state when it argued that "State legitimacy must ultimately be built on the foundations of democratic political practices and popular participation and engagement in matters of governance" (African Union Commission, 2004).

The above is in line with development experiences of the Nordic countries and some East Asian developmental states such as Japan. In fact, "[t]here is ample historical evidence that today's most advanced economies heavily relied on government intervention to ignite and facilitate their take-off and catch-up, which allowed them to build strong industrial bases and sustain their growth momentum over long periods" (Lin and Monga, 2010: 8). And to achieve these, they built and strengthened what Acemoglu and Robinson (2012) referred to as inclusive political and economic institutions. The ability of nations to foster inclusive development depends on the existence of enabling institutions, including legal and extra-legal rules that define property rights. They also include institutions such as the franchise, form of government (due process, rule of law), and coherent state institutions that are embedded in society that enables state and society to negotiate and renegotiate goals of development (Evans, 1995).

The highly acclaimed book of Acemoglu and Robinson (2012), *Why Nations Fail*, especially their discussion of inclusive political and economic institutions, is pertinent in this regard. This is because the creation of such institutions is critical if democratic governments in Nigeria want to foster industrial development and human capital expansion. Acemoglu and Robinson emphasised the complementarities between inclusive political institutions and inclusive economic institutions.

These acclaimed scholars observed that inclusive political institutions "are sufficiently centralised and pluralistic", in contrast to "extractive political institutions that concentrate power in the hands of a narrow elite and place few constraints on the exercise of this power" (Acemoglu and Robinson, 2012: 81). They went further to note that inclusive political institutions engender inclusive economic institutions because they vest power more broadly, which "would tend to uproot economic institutions that expropriate the resources of the many, erect entry barriers, and suppress the functioning of markets" (p. 82). Inclusive political and economic institutions will therefore be more conducive to promote human capital development in Nigeria and ultimately inclusive sustainable development—as elsewhere. This, in effect, calls for a democratic developmental state in Nigeria.

As has been recognised in the work on democratic developmental states, including the Nordic countries and Mauritius, three sets of capacities, namely, political, organisational and technical are critical for a state that is democratic and developmental to be able to undertake a process of structural transformation of an economy and expansion of human capabilities, that is, human capital development. This will ensure economic justice, which includes basic needs such as access to food, shelter, medical care, housing and quality and affordable education. Francis Fukuyama (2016) eloquently argued that public administration should be top priority for any country that wants to rise to the top. As he observed, "the biggest problems we face in contemporary governance are often not related to what the government should do, but rather how to actually get the existing machinery to implement a policy that everyone can agree upon" (Fukuyama, 2016: 1). The point, therefore, is not so much as getting the policy right, but getting the institutions right.   In fact, the development success or otherwise of the state is largely dependent on the functionality and capabilities of the public service.

Organisational capacity means the ability of the state to establish and nurture state institutions that act as collective and coherent entities. Central to organisational capacity is the establishment of planning agencies, which in the context of East Asian developmental states are referred to as superministries/agencies or coordinating agencies. Superministries ensure that policies and programmes of line ministries are in accordance with the overarching government development policies and programmes. In the case of the developmental states, these agencies dominate public policies, including economic policies. The Economic Planning Board (EPB), before its closure as part of the anti-state orientation of the Korean state since the 1990s, was a good example in this regard. As I noted elsewhere (2007: 133), "It had a broad mandate over planning, budgetary and economic management. This enabled it to ensure that government's policies, programmes and spending were synchronised, thereby avoiding an overheating of the economy."

Till today, the Economic Planning Unit (EPU) of Malaysia performs similar functions in spite of the fact that there is a Ministry of Finance. The former approves development projects, while the latter performs the treasury role of allocating the funds for projects approved by the EPU. Therefore, planning capacity is central to a democratic developmental state. This is complemented by technical capacity, which means that state agencies are staffed by qualified personnel. In particular, the planning agencies attract the best and brightest in society. As an example, in 2014, the Malaysian EPU had 330 staff, all of whom were graduates:

> Of these, 50% have masters degrees, and between 15-20% are PhD-holders. The main academic backgrounds of EPU's staff are Economics (most with economic background at postgraduate level), Business Administration (MBA) and Law. And because the EPU is responsible for approval of development projects, some of its staff have engineering backgrounds (engineers, architects, and quantity surveyors) – they vet the cost of projects before the Ministry of Finance allocates funds to them. Those with engineering backgrounds staff the Project Management Section of the unit (Public Service Commission, 2014b: 25 - 26).

The highly qualified personnel and other top bureaucrats constitute the elite corps of the civil service, and there is limited political interference in their work – ministers merely provide oversight.

Through both its organisational and technical capacities, the state is able to generate and analyse data. On the basis of these, the state is able to independently articulate and formulate a national development framework. Through its organisational and technical capacities, the state is able to develop and implement coherent National Development Plans (NDPs) and ensure effective coordination and allocation of resources. Furthermore, due to its internal capacities, both administrative and technical, the state is able to negotiate with non-state actors in the process of forging a joint project of national transformation. Its capacities engender trust (both functional and capability trusts) from business, CSOs and other non-state actors. As a result, non-state actors, including the private sector, see the state as a reliable partner. This points to the fact that democratic developmentalism requires a state that has a competent, capable, professional and career orientated bureaucracy.

One of the world's leading scholars of the democratic developmental state, Peter Evans aptly captured it thus:

> The internal organisations of the developmental state come much closer to approximating a Weberian bureaucracy. Highly selective meritocratic recruitment and long-term career rewards create a commitment and a sense of corporate coherence. Corporate coherence gives these apparatuses a certain kind of autonomy (Evans, 1995: 12).

It should be noted that democratic developmentalism lends itself to technocratic public policy. It requires bureaucrats who are competent, professional, disciplined, efficient and effective in the discharge of their duties. They provide advice to the executive and formulate and implement policies to meet the broad developmental goals set by political leaders. To effectively do this, the bureaucratic cadres have to be relatively insulated from direct pressure from interest groups and from "overt" political interference. But this is predicated on the political capacity of the state.

Jettisoning of Merit and Job Insecurity in the Nigerian Civil Service

How civil servants are recruited, and the security of their tenure are key determinants of the capacity of the state. These are critical elements in determining the efficiency of the state. Merit-based recruitment of civil servants through open, transparent and competitive entrance examinations is a necessary condition for human capability enhancement and economic growth. In other words, meritocracy is a key driver for structural transformation, inclusive growth and development. Similarly, predictable and rewarding career paths have similar effects. These are sources of state autonomy, which is a variable of the developmental state. The literature on the democratic developmental state has shown that the combination of a spoils/patronage recruitment system, and an unpredictable career path (job insecurity) for civil servants will have negative impacts on development.

Drawing from British tradition, Nigeria's founding fathers and mothers recognised this much when they argued for a merit-based system of recruitment and promotion of civil servants by independent bodies that were free from executive control and the need for permanence in their appointments. In this regard, it is pertinent to quote Mr E.O. Eyo, who took part in the 1953 constitutional negotiations of Nigeria. His eloquent rendition was that:

> The principle of the British system, which had stood the test of time, were that Civil Service was recruited by a body completely independent of ministers and has its own machinery for promotions, which except at the highest level, were not even submitted to Ministers for formal approval. Even when that approval was sought, Ministers were, by tradition, guided by the advice of senior members of the service. Finally, there was no question of the dismissal of the holders of offices in the Civil Service, at any level, in the consequence of a change of Government. In short, the British

tradition was that appointment and dismissal, and, with few exceptions, the promotions of civil servants, was outside the competence of Government. History showed that no other system works satisfactorily. It would be disastrous to have a civil service under the control of the Executive and for appointments to change according to the turn of the political wheel would lead to instability. In some countries, such a system had proved fatal (See Fika, 2014: 15).

This extensive quote highlights the principles that Nigeria's founding fathers and mothers felt should form the basis for public administration in the country. The aim is to show how subsequent departure from those principles, even under the democratic dispensation since 1999, has contributed to the country's poor development performance. The cohesiveness, productivity, performance and ultimately, the development of a nation suffers when the merit and security of tenure of civil servants are sacrificed for representativeness and patronage recruitment and promotion.

The immediate post-independent Nigerian civil service was based on merit. Recruitment was not through a patronage/spoils system, but through open, competitive entrance examinations. Civil servants were appointed on a permanent basis until retirement. Thus, they had security of tenure. A career civil servant could not be easily fired. Also, promotion was based on productivity and performance. But over time, the recruitment and promotion in the civil service became politicised, ethniticised and reflective of the preferences of influential members of society and on political affiliations.

According to a former Director General of the Bureau of Public Service Reforms, Dr Joe Abah, merit has been replaced with representativeness in the guise of a federal character in the civil service[17]. To illustrate this point, every state is required to have a permanent secretary in the federal civil service. The problem though is

---

[17]   *Author interview with Joe Abah. 23 March 2018.*

109   Nigeria: Democracy without Development. How to fix it

that some states have more directors than others. Directors from such states are bypassed for promotion in favour of, say a deputy director from a state with fewer representatives among the senior officers. Representativeness has thus trumped merit in the Nigerian civil service. As a result, the unpredictable career path and the promotion of some civil servants above their senior colleagues in the name of federal character demotivates overlooked colleagues. It also destroys the spirit of collegiality in the service. Ultimately, this has contributed to inefficiency in the civil service.

Table 3: Career progression in the Nigerian Civil Service

Level	Maturity	Cumulative Years in Service
8	3	3
9	3	6
10	3	9
12	3	12
13	3	15
14	4	19
15 (AD)	4	23
16 (DD)	4	27
17	8	35

Table 3 shows the levels and years that a civil servant is meant to spend at each level before promotion and the cumulative years in service. This shows that when a civil servant enters the service at entry level 8, he/she is expected to get to level 17 (Director) after having spent twenty-seven years in service. By the time he/she retires at the age of sixty years, they would have spent another eight years as either director or permanent secretary. The problem however is that in the name of representativity, otherwise known as federal character, some civil servants spend fewer years at one or more levels. Such civil servants become senior to their colleagues who entered the service at the same time. This violates one of the principles of the service: that promotion should be based on seniority.

As Dr Joe Abah observed, when a civil servant sits for a promotion examination, he/she is competing against those from his or her state.[18] Thus a civil servant from State A can score higher than his/her peers from State B, but the latter will be promoted in the name of representativity. Even the annual performance evaluation that constituted one of the factors for consideration for promotion has been corrupted as assessors tend to award higher marks to candidates from their areas. The second problem is that because some civil servants are promoted without spending the required years at one or more level, such civil servants spend more than the eight years required for both the position of director and permanent secretary. To overcome these problems, the "tenure" system was introduced in 2009, though with much resistance from some quarters.

To be appointed as a permanent secretary, a vacancy based on "state of origin" of the civil servant has to exist. To illustrate the point, if your state of origin is Kogi, you will only be appointed if no other civil servant from the state is a permanent secretary in the Federal Civil Service. Candidates are appointed to fill slots of their states. The examinations for permanent secretary level are conducted for the states, and the actual appointment to the position is made by the president to whom they owe their allegiance. Permanent secretaries are therefore political appointees, an inheritance from the military era. Also, some civil servants enter the service not at an entry level, but at managerial levels, that is, adverts for such positions are opened to those outside the service. Nigerian civil service is therefore not a classic Weberian bureaucracy that characterised developmental states, which requires that those at the core of bureaucracy must be employed at the entry level and can aspire to the highest position in the bureaucracy. In the Nigerian case, not all civil servants can become permanent secretaries because of their states of origin, and permanent secretaries

---

[18] *Author interview, 23 March 2018.*

are no longer career civil servants – in some instances permanent secretaries have been appointed from outside the service. In effect, civil servants do not have a predictable career path like in developmental states. This creates ill-will and destroys the sense of collegiality that is required for the efficiency of the bureaucracy. Suffice it to say that the politicisation of the civil service, including making permanent secretaries political appointees, is one of the banes of the Nigerian state. At the state level, the situation is worse because those from outside the public service can be appointed as permanent secretaries. This politicises the civil service. Inevitably, unpredictable career paths for civil servants in the country has created a fertile ground for corruption and inefficiency. It has also created a situation where a fraction of the time is spent actually doing their jobs, that is, most top civil servants are engaged in businesses other than that for which they were recruited. In fact, there are civil servants who work part time with their businesses as their main preoccupation.

Another problem facing the Nigerian civil service is that some civil servants pay millions of naira to be promoted and posted to "juicy positions". Thus, in addition to the violation of promotion being based on seniority, merit is compromised during promotion exercises. Furthermore, the promotion examination is not relevant to the competence required at the various levels. As Joe Abah pointed out, "There is a disconnect between the promotion examination and the competence required for the jobs. The examination focused more on the civil service rules[19]."

Clearly, appointments and promotions in the Nigerian civil service have, for a long time, depended on nepotism, tribalism and political patronage. At times, proponents of this turpitude present them under the guise of federal character. One of the consequences of the uncertain career path for civil servants is that they engage in private business while in service. These business interests are never disclosed. These public officials award contracts to their companies or their

---

[19] *Author interview, 23 March 2018.*

family members and friends in violation of the public procurement policy. This corrupts the civil service in particular and the state in general.

Engendering State Capture through Patronage/Spoils Recruitment Systems

Over the years, the spoils/patronage systems have characterised recruitment and promotion in the Nigerian public service. A popular online newspaper, *Sahara Reporters* (2016b) revealed that ninety-one relatives of influential Nigerians, including those of the President, former Vice President, Ministers, and Inspector General of Police were secretly employed by the Central Bank of Nigeria (CBN) without following established rules and regulations for employment in the public sector. The explanation by the CBN to another online newspaper, *Premium Times* (2016) that it was a "targeted recruitment" to pick "specialists" is alien to the process laid down for the recruitment of personnel into the public sector, which requires that recruitment is done in an open and transparent manner.

In fact, in violation of the rules, positions for recruitment into the CBN and the Nigerian National Petroleum Corporation (NNPC) are hardly advertised. Instead, the political and business elite, as well as prominent traditional leaders get their children and relatives recruited through the back door into these two important national institutions. This is the general trend in being recruited into the Nigerian civil service. As an example, in a letter dated December 27, 2017, the Kano Emirate Council requested the Chairman of the Federal Civil Service Commission to give favourable consideration to five applicants for employment in the service (see Appendix 1). According to a report by the United Nations Office on Drugs and Crime, *et al* (2019), 32.5% of successful applicants into the public service secured their jobs through bribery. It concludes that nepotism and bribery are the dominant means through which applicants are employed in the service.

113

Nigeria: Democracy without Development. How to fix it

In general, slots are given to governors, members of the National Assembly, State Houses of Assembly, ministers, family members, heads of service at state and federal levels, commissioners and top officials of the federal civil service commission, traditional and religious leaders, leaders of political parties, and so on. To illustrate this point, at the screening of ministerial nominees submitted by President Buhari to the Senate for his second term, Senator Remi Tinubu complained to Babatunde Fashola (Minister for Works, Power and Housing in Buhari's first term) that he should:

> ...remember I didn't get any chance to give employment letter to my constituency... So, when you get there this time, just remember senators here that have people back home. My constituents are asking us for employment slots. So, I want you to put that in your agenda for next tenure...We all need slots for employment for our constituents (Channels TV, July 2019).

This is a classic case of the political elite seeing themselves as employment agencies, dispensing jobs to families, friends and those in their good books. This is one means by which the Nigerian state is captured. As Lodge (2018: 16) observed, "exercising complete control over civil service appointments" is one means to capture the state.

The adverse effects on national development because of the lack of meritocratic recruitment and long-term reward and predictable career paths are profound. The former Minister of the Federal Capital Territory, Nasir Ahmad El-Rufai (2013: 90), who led the public service reforms in the second half of President Olusegun Obasanjo's second term, illustrates in his book *The Accidental Public Servant* the impact this had on Nigeria's development. According to him, when civil servants realised that their jobs were no longer secure, they came to the conclusion that they had to feather their nests, that is, to use the state as a means of personal wealth accumulation.

Nigeria: Democracy without Development. How to fix it

114

Also, unlike the 1960s and '70s, Nigeria's best and the brightest no longer aspire to a career in the public service. This is largely as a result of the perversion of recruitment, promotions and postings (which are bought and sold) coupled with the poor remuneration of civil servants, which is about 75% lower than in the private sector. The public service, El-Rufai observed, has lost its prestige as the first port of call for the brightest Nigerian graduates. This has had adverse effects on the Nigerian state. Rules and procedures are observed in the breach and consequently, the state lacks a sense of corporate identity as public servants become beholden to individuals or outside interests who ensured their recruitment, promotions and postings. As a result, the Nigerian state has become dysfunctional. In such a context, the state will be unable to pursue any collective goals. In fact, the Nigerian state has limited capacity to provide public goods to citizens and to stimulate the structural transformation of the economy[20].

The point is that when recruitment is based on political patronage, coupled with uncertain career paths, senior bureaucrats are unable to take a long-term view of social and economic development. As a result, they will be unable to devise the right policy tools to transform their economies and promote inclusive sustainable development. Therefore, rather than foster a growth path that will enhance a country's productive capacities, bureaucrats (hand-in-glove with politicians) have engaged in conspicuous consumption. Clearly, the Nigerian state lacks the institutional capacity to regulate such perverted behaviour.

The patronage/spoils system that characterises recruitment into the Nigerian civil service and other state agencies clearly undermines democratic principles, including that of equality of opportunity and social justice. As Elster (1992) correctly observed, "justice requires fair equality of opportunity concerning access to positions in society – for example, jobs, entrance to schools and universities, positions in

---

[20] *This paragraph and the next are lifted from the concept paper titled "Towards a conceptual framework for a developmental state in South Africa", which I prepared for the South African Public Service Commission in 2013.*

government..." (Elster, 1992, cited in Little, 2003: 101). But in a captured states like Nigeria, "the state ... lost its social autonomy and is unable to function in such a way as to serve broad social interests or to make decisions that might achieve long-term developmental goals. It is unable to do these things because it has become harnessed to a very particular and especially narrow set of private interests" (Lodge, 2018: 14).

A good example in this regard is Nigeria's inability to enact a comprehensive law to regulate and govern the oil and gas sector, which as we noted earlier is the main source of government revenue. Fifteen years after the formulation of the (NOGP) National Oil and Gas Policy (2005), upon which the Petroleum Industry Bill (PIB), and subsequent Act was to be anchored, successive administrations are yet to enact a comprehensive law to regulate and govern the sector. This is due in part to the role of the International Oil Companies (IOCs) that have frustrated efforts to pass such a law, and that even if one is passed, their interests must be considered paramount. In our assessment of the twelfth draft of the PIB, which we subsequently presented to the parliamentary ad-hoc committee on the bill, we observed that as follows:

> We still find that the narrow interests of the petroleum industry predominate, and the protection of these interests has actually improved as we move from the NOGP to the Bill draft. In short, the draft of the bill has improved the interests of the petroleum industry (from 50 to 64%, or an increase of 14%), at the expense of Nigerian producers (-16%), and with only a slight improvement (2%) for the interests of the Nigerian people at large. It is clear that the Bill leans heavily in the direction of protecting the interests of the international petroleum industry (Edigheji, *et al.*, 2013).

According to the global extractive industry watchdog, *Publish What You Pay* (PWYP), "Nigeria is losing ₦3 trillion annually for failing to put in place proper legislation for the oil and gas industry" (*Vanguard*,

2018). In addition, jobs are being lost because of the non-passage of the law. This is an illustration of the adverse effects of state capture, which as noted earlier, makes it impossible for the state to take autonomous action to advance national interests.

The spoils/patronage system has given rise to the phenomenon of "ghost workers" at all levels (local government, state and federal) in the Nigerian civil service. Ghost workers are people who may or may not exist but whose names are added to the public service payroll. Fraudulent public servants – politicians and civil servants – collect the salaries of these ghost workers every month. This costs the country billions of naira each year. According to President Muhammadu Buhari, his administration discovered "forty-three thousand ghost workers through the Integrated Payroll and Personnel Information System. That represents pay packets totalling ₦4.2 billion stolen every month" (Buhari, 2016). The number of ghost workers at the federal level rose to about 60,000 but with the continued computerisation of the payroll, and when matched with Bank Verification Numbers (BVNs), it exposed 23,000 people collecting multiple salaries. This situation is just as pervasive at states and local government levels.

The administration of Governor Nasir Ahmad El-Rufai in Kaduna State discovered over 13,000 ghost workers (*Punch*, 2016) that cost the state six billion naira per year. At the local government level in the state, the administration discovered 2,087 ghost workers through the biometric verification exercise it carried out. Similarly, in Delta State, the administration of Governor Ifeanyi Okowa, through its biometric exercise discovered and removed from the payroll about 26,000 ghost workers in 2018 (*Daily Post*, 2018). At the local government level, the Bayelsa State Government discovered 28,000 ghost workers on the payroll of its eight local government areas (see *Premium Times*, 2018). This shows that the phenomenon of ghost workers is widespread in the country.

These fraudulent practices are perpetuated by politicians, civil servants and at times traditional rulers. They continue in the absence of biometric data verification of civil servants. It is civil servants that collect these multiple salaries. In a particularly notorious instance, the biometric data verification implemented by the Buhari administration through Bank Verification Numbers (BVNs) revealed that one civil servant was collecting twenty salaries.

What the above shows is that the method of recruitment is an important analytical starting point to understand the efficiency and capacity of the state. When employment into the public service is based on a patronage/spoils system, it breeds corruption and hampers the capacity of the state to pursue a development agenda. It is also directly correlated with increases in inequality. For instance, about 70% of the Nigerian budget goes to recurrent expenditure, most of which is for salaries. In this context when one civil servant fraudulently collects the salaries of twenty people, it increases the concentration of income and wealth in few individuals. Inequality is further exacerbated when only children and relatives of politicians, top bureaucrats and captains of industries are employed in the public service.

Furthermore, there is an interesting trend in the country, where children of the elite marry amongst themselves, ensuring the elite also have informal institutional networks among themselves. But unlike other development contexts where such informal institutional arrangements complement the formal institutional arrangement to propel development, as argued by Evans (1995), in the Nigerian case, these informal networks are built on consumption and pillage of the commonwealth, rather than on productivity. These informal networks add limited value to national wealth creation but contribute to the concentration of wealth in a few families.

The phenomenon of ghost workers in the public service has a number of adverse implications for national development. For one, it increases the cost of governance. Also, funds that could have been invested in productive and income generating activities, infrastructural development and measures to address poverty are stolen by a few individuals. In addition, jobs-for-cash results in the provision of poor quality service to citizens. Furthermore, when funds meant for provision of public goods are stolen, citizens are denied such services. Lastly, ghost workers also undermine the legitimacy of government.

The Weberian attribute of a long-term rewarding career (with employment until retirement) that characterised the civil service in the immediate post-independence period has been jettisoned in the country. The first jolt to the system occurred in the 1970s, when in one fell swoop, the General Murtala Mohammad military regime retired thousands of civil servants. Also, in 1988 under military rule, ministers assumed not just the powers of appointment, promotion and discipline over public servants, but the supervisory role permanent secretaries had over civil servants as well, policies which eventually ended career public service in the real sense of the word. These changes put an end to the golden age of the Nigerian civil service. Furthermore, those actions have had corrosive effects on the public service: job insecurity, corruption, indiscipline, impunity, etc.

The Nigerian civil service has not recovered from the onslaught. Almost forty years after the military dismantled its Weberian attributes, the civil service is still being eroded in the democratic era commencing in 1999. As an example, those in administrative leadership positions, such as permanent secretaries, are prematurely retired when a new administration comes to power. As noted earlier, permanent secretaries have become political appointees. In some instances, including at the sub-national level, permanent secretaries are appointed from outside the civil service. The Nigerian case is unlike countries such as Malaysia, India, Mauritius, Singapore, China and South Korea, to name just a few that continue to have a merit-based career public service. In these countries, career public servants are appointed on a permanent basis until retirement. This is an inheritance from British colonial rule. Thus, public servants in these countries have security of tenure. A career civil servant cannot be easily fired and a change of government does not affect or result in the dismissal and retirement of career civil servants. In fact, in most democracies, with the exception of the US and Italy, there is minimum political involvement in staffing issues. These include the Nordic countries of Sweden and Denmark.

Non-merit-based systems and non-career public services have other adverse consequences for the state. It institutionalises corruption in the system. All of these have given rise to a situation where public servants are among the richest people in the country. In fact, the Nigerian state has become an avenue of wealth accumulation by elected officials, political appointees and civil servants. The system lends credence to corruption, as civil servants are poorly paid and are not able to maintain chosen lifestyles from their legitimate income. Civil servants use their period in the service to enrich themselves and this becomes more urgent given the lack of security of tenure. In addition, non-merit-based recruitment brings about inefficiency in the public service and destroys the e*spirit de corps* that is essential for its efficient functioning. Worse still, in such a context, their loyalty is to their patrons, not to the state. This creates personality cults. Therefore, the Nigerian state is unable to act as a collective and coherent entity.

Also, the spoils/patronage system not only engenders indiscipline in the public service but also demoralises public servants. The civil service has since ceased to be an effective instrument for the implementation of government policies. As an example, the lack of implementation capacity cannot be dissociated from the lack of merit-based recruitment and promotion in the public service. Similarly, the problem of state capture and corruption in the democratic era is strongly positively correlated with the absence of a merit-based public service and job insecurity of civil servants. Reflecting on the effect of this, one of the most experienced civil servants in Nigeria, Baba Gana Kingibe (2013: 6) concluded that, "The legitimacy of power and authority and the internal maintenance of the rule of law which were inherent dimensions of its rationale and functionality were …

compromised."

Corruption has other adverse implications on the country's development. Crucially, resources that are meant for social and economic development are diverted into private use thus depriving citizens of access to basic social services. In addition, there are limited resources to invest in physical infrastructure and consequently the basic economic infrastructure remains inadequate and poor. Also, corruption serves as a disincentive for citizens to pay taxes. It is therefore no surprise that of the 77.6 million economically active people in Nigeria, only 19 million were tax compliant in 2018, according to erstwhile Minister of Finance, Kemi Adeosun (2018a). Consequently, the Nigerian tax to GDP ratio is abysmal: at only 6%, it is one of the lowest in the world.

Furthermore, because the patronage/spoils system is the dominant means of recruitment and promotion in the public service, the best and brightest Nigerians are not in the service. This partly accounts for the low productivity and poor service delivery of civil servants. Left to their own devises, civil servants are not able to generate enough revenue to cover their salaries. These unproductive and inefficient civil servants consume a substantial share of the nation's revenue. To give an instance, at the federal level, there are 82,000 personnel. This small number consumes about 70% of the national budget. At the sub-national level, Kaduna State with a population of about 9,000,000 people spent over 90% of its revenue on 87,000 civil servants as at May 2015[21]. With increased overhead costs, there are inadequate funds for capital expenditure that will change the economy and provide infrastructure to its people. In fact, Nigeria in the democratic era does not meet the international norm when 70% of the country's budget is expended on capital related activities. Though the Buhari administration is increasing its capital expenditure, it still falls below the international norm. The infrastructural deficit is estimated to cost about $3 trillion.

---

[21] *This includes both the state and 23 local government's civil servants. However, Governor El-Rufai has changed this situation with 70 – 30 ratio of the state expenditure on capital and recurrent budget.*

The lack of capacity of the organisational and administrative structures of the state to provide basic services to citizens and the pervasive corruption in the public sector delegitimises democracy. Citizens lose confidence in democratic governance. Citizens need democratic dividends and want to be sure that public servants will be above board in the discharge of their duties and do so impartially.

Weak technical, administrative and political capacities have given room to state capture and corruption. Though for a different period (1970 – 1990), the data for Weberian bureaucratic structures and planning ministries as the most important state bureaucracy, in a sample of twelve developing countries, shows that Nigeria had one of lowest degrees of autonomy. This reflected the fact that recruitment into the civil service was based on patronage and civil servants had no predictable career path. In addition, they lacked planning and coordinating capacities (Edigheji, 2007). As demonstrated in this book, this situation has not changed significantly since the mid-1990s under democratic governments. The low degree of autonomy of the Nigerian state offers fertile ground for corruption.

In a corrupt environment, as Samura (2009) rightly noted, "The real development priorities of a country are often neglected in favour of those that generate the greatest personal gains for decision-makers *and those of their patrons*" (*emphasis added*). In fact, this creates a climate for state capture by powerful interests, both national and international. Furthermore, the merging of the Ministry of Planning and Budget with the Ministry of Finance on August 21, 2019 by President Buhari in his second term is likely to have a corroding effect on planning. This is because the focus of the new ministry is likely to be on ensuring macroeconomic stability rather than development planning.

As noted earlier, Nigerian politicians and senior bureaucrats are amongst the richest people in the country due to massive corruption. They live a life of luxury while their constituents continue to wallow in squalor and poverty. Therefore, like under military rule, most of the

Nigerian political class and bureaucratic elite in the democratic dispensation seem content to live on rent from oil. They therefore have no incentives to diversify the country's economy, a point that is clearly highlighted in Figure 2.

The poor management of the economy by successive governments is however not surprising because it has not been in the interest of the rent-seeking elites and *tenderpreneurs* to manage oil resources for shared prosperity and to lay a foundation for a post-oil Nigerian economy. It is therefore not by accident that there is no structural transformation of the economy to shift focus to high value-added services and manufacturing.

Amnesty International (AI) made the connection between corruption and human rights violation and the erosion of democracy when it argued that "corruption undermines human rights and, often, binds state agents to corporate interests, removing the state's motive and capacity to protect human rights" (Amnesty International, 2014: 173). AI went further to show that where there are conflicts between the company's interests in affected communities, governments have been predisposed to favour corporate interests, as has been the case in the Niger Delta. The crisis between the Ogoni people and Shell is an apt example. Such conflicts have had negative environmental impacts that in some cases destroyed the livelihood of local communities. Overall, this has led to climate change that threatens our world and common humanity. Furthermore, without billions of illicit financial flows from the continent, Africa will have very little need to depend on foreign aid. The point was poignantly captured by Nigeria's erstwhile Minister of Finance, Kemi Adeosun in a tweet on February 20, 2018 when she observed that, "If Multinational Corporations stopped exploiting countries like Nigeria through tax malpractices and other illicit financial flows, there probably wouldn't be a need for foreign aid. The revenues from blocking these malpractices would render aid unnecessary" (Adeosun, 2018b). She called these "foreign corruption practices".

Chapter Five

Towards a Shared and Prosperous Future: Building a Democratic Developmental State in Nigeria

History and development theory support the proposition "no developmental state, no development." The idea of a developmental state puts robust, competent public institutions at the center of the developmental matrix.

Peter Evans (2010)

Introduction

I t is argued earlier in this book that liberal democracy has normative values and is worth pursuing and celebrating in its own right. While there is no doubt that Nigeria has embraced democracy and some progress has been made, electoral democracy remains unstable for reasons that have been elaborated earlier. Part of the progress is that for the first time in its history, the country has experienced the longest period of uninterrupted civilian rule of twenty years. There have now been four successive administrations: President Olusegun Obasanjo (29 May 1999 – 29 May 2017), President Umaru Musa Yar'Adua (29 May 2007 – 5 May 2010), President Goodluck Jonathan (5 May 2010 – 29 May 2015) and President Muhammadu Buhari (29 May 2015 – current). The country had its sixth multi-party and regular democratic elections in February and March 2019.

Also, there has been a peaceful transfer of power from one civilian administration to another – from President Jonathan of the PDP to President Buhari of the APC. The country has also recorded improved scores in the areas of civil and political liberties. The introduction of card readers in the 2015 elections reduced the brazen rigging that characterised previous elections and the Independent National Electoral Commission, from the period of Professor Attahiru Jega as chairman, has become relatively more independent (although it faced difficult challenges under the chairmanship of Professor Mahmood Yakubu during the 2019 General Elections). All of these bode well for the survival of liberal democracy in the country.

Developmentalism in Nigeria: Poor Performance of the Political Elite

As noted earlier, it is important to analyse democracy through the prism of developmentalism – the ability to improve livelihoods, promote social justice, promote high wage employment, reduce poverty and inequality, promote inclusive development, and engender industrial development and other high valued added economic activities. The analysis in this book shows that democracy in Nigeria is failing to deliver social and economic development because it is built on flawed foundations – market fundamentalism and weak state capacities. In the last twenty years, the electoral system and its socio-economic outcomes have been rigged against a majority of the Nigerian populace. This is primarily due to both the exclusionary political and economic institutions that cater for the interests of the elite.

Lack of Political and Administrative Capacity

In general, the Nigerian state lacks the political and administrative capacities to formulate and implement policies for industrial development, and to promote economic and social inclusion. This is why successive administrations in the democratic era have not been able to diversify the economy in any meaningful way. The diversification of the economy in the democratic era has had minimum impact on development because it has occurred predominantly in low value-added services and the agriculture sectors, with the oil and gas sector remaining the main source of government revenue.

Though the service sector has become the highest contributor to GDP, it is not contributing much to the creation of decent jobs (agriculture and the informal sectors remain the largest employment creators) and livelihoods. This is happening in the context of small industrial and manufacturing sectors. The diversification of the Nigerian economy, with the service sector becoming the largest contributor to GDP, is unlike development experiences elsewhere – America and Europe, and more recently the Asian developmental states such as China and South Korea – that started with strong and large manufacturing sector that served as necessary foundations upon which their service sectors were built. Hence, in those countries, the service sector created high-value activities that propelled economic growth and global competitiveness, as well as major sources of foreign exchange earnings. Unlike the Nigerian situation, the comparative cases created high wage employment because their service sectors included high value-added service sectors. Consequently, their service sectors had positive multiplier effects in the value chain of the sector and the rest of their economies.

Untransformed Structure of the Nigerian Economy and Continued Dependence on Oil

While the Nigerian economy grew at 6.1% on average in 18 years between 2000 and 2017, the growth has been due to increases in global oil prices rather than due to any concerted programmes pursued by the political elite. Consequently, the economy remains vulnerable to the volatility of global oil prices. Following the decline in global oil prices, which started in June 2014, the Nigerian economy's growth rate began to decline in the fourth quarter of the same year and subsequently went into recession in 2016.

Underinvestment in Human Capital and Exclusionary Economic Outcomes

It has been shown in this book that successive administrations in the democratic dispensation (16 years under the PDP and 4 years under the APC) have under-invested in people, the main asset of the country, who should be the main drivers of development. Consequently, poverty, inequality, unemployment and underemployment have consistently increased since 1999. The high levels of poverty, unemployment and hunger in the country are stripping citizens of their humanity and dignity. What this shows is that liberal democracy has not served the interests of the people. A majority of Nigerians have no access to quality education and healthcare, and there is no significant social protection. Also, most households have no access to electricity and potable water. In all, the Nigerian state during the democratic dispensation, like during military rule, has not been able to foster economic and social inclusion. Instead, the 20 years of electoral democracy has been marked by an economy that worked for the wealthy few, while at the same time increased the number of Nigerians living below the poverty line. Unemployment and underemployment have also increased. It is therefore safe to conclude that Nigeria is neither democratic nor developmental. It is not a fluke that the credibility of electoral democracy is being eroded.

The political elite have shown total disregard for the education sector, the most potent weapon for peace, freedom, change, innovation, liberation from oppression, and a tool for every human being to fulfill their potential. As the late Kofi Annan put it, "Education is a right with immense power to transform. On its foundation rest the cornerstone of freedom, democracy and sustainable human development; and it is the premise of progress, in every society, in every family" (Annan, 1999: 4). By implication, the neglect of education and the under-investment in the education sector by the political and administrative elites are not only violations of human rights but also a trampling on the very foundation of democracy. Also, the neglect has compromised the future of Nigerians and the progress and prosperity of the country. This will have adverse generational impact not only on citizens but on the development and global ranking of Nigeria.

Ideological Poverty of the Political Elite and Exclusionary Socio-economic Outcomes

The fact that electoral democracy has not delivered an inclusive economy or social justice is partly due to the ideological poverty of the political elite, who are driven by self-interest rather than service to citizens and the nation. Lacking the ideology of development nationalism, the political class has been unable to transform the structure of the economy to give premium to high value-added economic activities and to invest in the people of Nigeria to enhance their wellbeing.

One area that underscores the ideological poverty and lack of capacity of the Nigerian political class in 20 years of electoral democracy is power generation. Africa's richest person, Aliko Dangote (2019) poignantly captured the crisis thus: "In Nigeria, we have been struggling for 18 years without adding 1,000 megawatts and we have spent about three times above Egypt, why?" In contrast, "Egypt increased its electricity by 10 gigawatts, which is equivalent to 10,000 megawatts in 18 months." As Dangote rightly pointed out, without electricity, there can be no economic growth. In the same vein, without electricity, the enhancement of human wellbeing is compromised. This is in spite of President Obasanjo's administration reportedly spending $16 billion on electricity. What is clear is that this amount went into the pockets of individuals, with nothing to show for it. Pillaging the commonwealth and compromising the national interest have been the dominant preoccupation of the political elite. As a result, corruption has become a blight on constitutional democracy.

In the absence of an ideology of development nationalism, the political elite have failed to build the technical and organisational capacity of the state to drive developmentalism. As shown in this book, it explains the fact that the dominant political parties in the country are not ideologically driven. Also, they do not function as organisations as there are no explicit collective goals that keep members together, beyond using them as vehicles for politicians to achieve self-enrichment and willful domination of other citizens.

Lack of Internal Party Democracy, Impunity of Politicians and Corruption of Recruitment of Political Leaders

The main political party that ruled the country for 16 years was unable to manage its own affairs. The party lack independence. Under

President Obasanjo in particular, the PDP was an extension of the presidency, with the president dictating to the party what to do. This created instability within the party. The headline in *Premium Times* of January 24, 2014 captures it thus "How PDP disgraced six of its seven chairmen in 15 years". In this period, none of its chairmen completed their tenures. It was reported that, in the case of Audu Ogbe, President Obasanjo forced him to resign as party chairman at gun point (*Premium Times*, 2018).

At the state level, political parties are run as extensions of the Governor's Office. They lack independence, and in-between elections, party structures exist only in name. Also, internal rancour, factionalisation and fights over how to choose their leaders and nominate candidates for elective public offices have been some of the major problems facing the party. For example, after the 2015 General Elections, PDP had two factional leaders, one led by Ahmed Makarfi as Chairman and the other by Ali Modu Sheriff. This division within the PDP was also evident at the various state levels. In Ogun State as an example, there was the Ladi Adebutu faction and the Senator Buruji Kashamu faction.

For its part, the inability of the APC to manage the nomination of those seeking elective positions and divisions within its state structures was laid bare in the period leading to the 2019 General Elections. This cost the party the governorship elections in states like Adamawa, Bauchi, Zamfara and Oyo that, on face value, it could have won. The dominant political parties in Nigeria are currently factionalised from ward to national levels. There are ongoing court cases between various factions of these political parties, such as between Cyril Ogodo and Jones Erue of the APC as to who the authentic leader of the party in Delta State is. Also, there is a public feud between the former chairman of the APC, Chief John Odigie-Oyegun and the current chairman, Comrade Adams Oshiomole, with the former accusing the latter of lacking capacity to manage the party, whom he said, "engages his mouth before engaging his mind."

According to him, "Oshiomhole is degrading the party. Rather(sic) than seek and bring more people on board, he is rather chasing people out of the party with his *agbero* style engagement". Specifically, he points to what he refers to as the "unfairness and injustices meted to many party members during the primaries process" (*Vanguard*, 2019). Odigie-Oyegun also alleged that Oshiomole's poor management skills was responsible for the party losing the 2019 elections in some states. In turn, the six South-South geo-political zone chairmen who support Comrade Oshiomhole blamed Chief Odigie-Oyegun for being responsible for the problems facing the APC. The current Deputy National Chairman of the party (North), Senator Lawan Shuaibu, joined the fray by calling for the resignation of Comrade Oshiomhole as Chairman. He accused him of incompetence and running the party without recourse to the National Working Committee (NWC) – the highest decision-making body that runs the party on daily basis. All these examples point to the poor management of political parties in the Fourth Republic.

Unprincipled Politicians: Implications for Democracy and Development

The majority of Nigerian politicians in the Fourth Republic are unprincipled and indisciplined. They are prepared to do anything to seize party structures and state power, and consequently thrive on amoral politics. An example is Senator Bukola Saraki, who connived with senators of the minority party, the PDP, to become the Senate President of the 8th Assembly[22] . Throughout his tenure, Senator Saraki[23] undermined his party, APC - the platform on which he was

---

[22] *When the 8th Senate was inaugurated, most APC Senators were not present because they were attending a caucus meeting called by President Buhari and the APC leadership.*
[23] *The phenomenon of senate presidents having running battles with the executive arm of government in the twenty years of democracy is not peculiar to Senator Saraki. His case is however, unique because he was installed as Senate President with the support of the official opposition party, the PDP, and throughout his tenure he conducted himself as the leader of the opposition to President Buhari's administration.*

elected. In addition, he became an obstructionist to the administration of President Buhari. In an audio recording that was circulated on social media, Senator Saraki was heard boasting that he was obstructing the administration of Buhari because he was not allowed to nominate people for appointments. He gleefully boasted about cutting the budgets for capital projects such as the construction of the Lagos-Ibadan Expressway by ₦30 billion. While signing the 2018 budget, President Buhari lamented that "The National Assembly made cuts amounting to 347 billion naira allocations to 4,700 projects submitted to them *by the administration* for consideration and introduced 6,403 projects of their own amounting to 578 billion naira" (Buhari, 2018, *emphasis added*). The cuts were for critical infrastructure while the projects inserted by NASS were those of little national significance. According to President Buhari, the inserted projects were "not properly conceptualised, designed and costed..."

Inordinate ambition, indiscipline and value-free politics explain why politicians cross carpet from one party to the other when a political party no longer serves to advance their personal, political and economic interests. The defections are destabilising not only to the political parties but also for constitutional democracy, as well as the country. The current democratic experiment has witnessed the deification by politicians of self-interest, especially money, at the expense of national development. Since 1999, Nigeria has been mal-governed by a political class that has consistently devalued the constitutional democratic order through their egregious abuse of political power. Public funds meant for basic services and the development of physical infrastructure are diverted to the bank accounts of politicians, their relatives and collaborators in the private sector. The case of the Niger Delta states discussed earlier, where up to 80% of all government revenues and budgetary allocations were reported to have been diverted to private use, exemplifies the degree of corruption in the country. These have generated resentment among citizens and the consequent decline in citizens' participation in elections. In the 1999 Presidential Election, voter turnout was 52.3%. In 2003 turnout rose to 69.1%. Since then, there has been a declining trend, 57.3% in 2007, 55.4% in 2011, 42.4% in 2015[24] with the 2019 General Elections experiencing the lowest voter turnout of about 35.6% (Centre for Democracy and Development, 2019).

Specifically, out of the 84 million registered voters, only 28.6 million voters turned out in the Presidential Elections of February 2019 – 11.2 million registered voters did not collect their Permanent Voters Cards (PVCs). The declining voter turnout is partly due to a lack of trust in Nigerian politicians by the citizenry. The apt words of Cardinal Onaiyekan provide a succinct description of the situation, when he observed that:

> We see this clearly in our country, Nigeria. We hear politicians often speaking about serving the nation. It has now become a huge joke. Even the simplest village man knows that the people in authority are not serving us. This is the major cause of our problems. Rulers become dictators instead of servants of ... the people (Onaiyekan, 2018: 1).

This book has highlighted the deterioration of the quality of political leadership in the country since 1999. The evocation of religious and ethnic sentiments by the political class has worsened divisions along these cleavages and thus undermined nation-building. Overcoming these challenges requires that developmentalists come together to form DCs to engage in the political process. The emergence of DCs is a necessary condition for national unity and a re-booting of the economy.

---

[24] *The percentage of voters turnout rates for the elections prior to the 2015 elections when card readers were introduced are doubtful because elections were characterised by massive rigging including snatching of ballot boxes, and politicians working in connivance with elections officials just writing and inflating elections results. This period can be described as "democracy without citizens" where politicians had total disregard for the wishes of voters. Some sanity has been brought to the electoral process with the introduction of card readers, reducing the level of rigging. But even with the introduction of card readers, politicians still devise ways to rig elections. This includes intimidation of electoral officials, especially the ad-hoc staff, some of whom are not properly trained to enforce the electoral laws and rules.*

Exclusionary Politics and Non-Inclusive Development

It has been shown that electoral democracy in the country has not been inclusive and failed to accommodate diversity, both in terms of gender and generational representations, because major decision-making structures are dominated by older males. In fact, there is structural discrimination against women in the Nigerian political system. Intimidation, thuggery, violence and money are some of the factors that work against women emerging as candidates for elective positions and subsequently being elected to public offices. An electoral process that has structural impediments against the election of women to leadership positions is not a democracy. Consequently, social and economic outcomes are disproportionately in favour of males and old people. One of the ways to change this situation is for a constitutional amendment that specifies equal representation of women in political parties and elective and appointive positions at all levels of government. Nigeria can take a cue from South Africa, Rwanda and more recently Ethiopia that have gender parity in their cabinets: 50% of ministers in Rwanda and Ethiopia are women, while women make up about 49% of ministers in South Africa.

Conclusion: Towards a Shared and Prosperous Future

For Nigeria to overcome these development and institutional deficits, it is proposed that democratic governments embrace developmentalism as an overarching national development agenda. In effect, development needs to be carried out democratically, in the context of an overarching endogenous national development plan and anchored on a long term national development vision. Its key elements should consist of the promotion of human capital development, infrastructural development and industrialisation.

Industrialisation, as a central element of ideology of development nationalism, will contribute to the structural transformation of the economy, create jobs and ultimately improve livelihoods. In this regard, agriculture-focused industrialisation should be given due attention. Also, the service sector needs to be anchored on a strong industrial sector for the former to make meaningful contributions to an inclusive economy. At the same time, pursuing high value-added services should be undertaken if the country is to reap the benefits of the digital age. Surely, attention needs to be given to the manufacturing sector if Nigeria is to transit from a country of consumers to that of producers of finished goods. Towards this end, in its relationship with countries of the Global South, Nigeria should promote the "flying geese" model, which will require that developing countries such as China, Brazil, South Korea, India, and so on, shift their simpler forms of manufacturing activities to Nigeria as they advance into more high value added manufacturing and services. This in turn will have a number of positive multiplier effects – increased employment, exports and domestic savings in Nigeria. The Vice President of the African Development Bank, Celestin Monga (2019) made the same point when he argued that:

> ...the primary goal of an effective growth-enhancing, job-creating strategy should be to lift the ... people now in low productivity or subsistence activities into industry, including agro-industrial business and some tradable services. Manufacturing provides more long-term economic benefits than other activities. It generates economies of scale, sparks industrial and technological upgrading, fosters innovation, and has big multiplier effects, with each factory requiring accountants, marketing people, component suppliers, restaurants, and other services (Monga, 2019: 2).

The positive multiplier effects will include creating decent jobs that will lift millions of people out of poverty and generate foreign exchange. Thus, while the Nigerian state promotes the agricultural and service sectors, these should be anchored on a strong manufacturing base. Nigeria ought to also take advantage of the fact that countries such as China are moving their light manufacturing to countries of the Global South. Government therefore needs to create the necessary infrastructure, including power, and other conditions conducive for investment, such as the ease of doing business, curbing corruption and tackling the challenges of insecurity. This will require partnerships with the private sector and civil society. In light of the adverse effects of climate change, government should give due consideration to greening the manufacturing sector to preserve the earth and create a shared future.

I have argued that developmentalism must be undertaken in the context of democracy. However, electoral democracy is a necessary but insufficient condition for Nigeria to overcome its development deficits of high unemployment and underemployment, a high level of poverty and inequality and dependence on the oil and gas sector as the main source of government revenue and foreign exchange earnings. This over dependence on oil and gas, as we observed above, makes it vulnerable to the volatility of the global economy.

This book has highlighted the necessity for a democratic developmental state in the country. Its critical elements include building the political, technical, organisational and administrative capacities of the state. Political capacity will be derived from political leadership that imbibes the ideology of development nationalism. The need for human capability expansion and development to overcome underdevelopment and catch up with other nations should be the overarching objective of political leaders. This calls for political parties in the country to be ideologically-based to enable citizens decide who to vote for, unlike the current situation where voters vote based on personalities, ethnicity and religion. Ideologically-based political parties are a *sine qua non* to the nation-building project and for developmentalism.

To achieve their development objectives, political leaders need to ensure bureaucratic efficiency and competence by building and deploying technical and organisational administrative capacities to enable the state achieve its developmental objectives. These are key variables for a democratic developmental state. To achieve this, recruitment and promotion in the civil service must be based on merit rather than patronage, religion and ethnicity. A meritocratic bureaucracy is a necessary condition for development. Also, the security of tenure of civil servants needs to be promoted and upheld to guarantee the professionalism and capability of the bureaucracy. Building an efficient and professional bureaucracy would require attracting the best and brightest into the corps of civil servants. Consequently, primacy should be given to merit in the recruitment and promotion of civil servants, while being cognisant of federal character. However, there is a need to end the perversion of the federal character whereby politicians, businesspeople, traditional rulers and religious leaders populate the public service with their wards through non-transparent and non-competitive processes.

Promotion in the civil service needs to be linked to performance. Key performance areas (which are national priorities) that promotion should be linked to are economic development, innovation and technological development, enhancement of human wellbeing and governance. In fact, ministers should sign performance-based contracts with the president and should be assessed at least quarterly. Here, the president and other states governors should take a cue from the governor of Kaduna state, Nasir El-Rufai, who in his second term made his political appointees, including commissioners, sign performance-based contracts. Ministers and civil servants who fail to meet their Key Performance Indicators (KPIs) in a year should be relieved of their posts. This is necessary to ensure the efficiency of the Nigerian state. The success of this requires the establishment of a strong performance management mechanism, as well as an efficient monitoring and evaluation system.

Furthermore, building a democratic development state would require enhancing the planning capacity of the Nigerian state to ensure greater coordination of government projects and programmes. In this regard, repositioning the Ministry of National Planning would be a critical element to enhance the capacity of the state – it needs to become the government think-tank with adequate human resources. As a first step, it should revert to its old name, National Planning Commission (NPC) and it should operate as a separate and independent entity from the Ministry of Finance. Like its counterparts, the National Development and Reforms Commission (NDRC), China and the Economic Planning Unit (EPU) Malaysia, it should recruit high-calibre technocrats into its rank. This will enhance its analytical, planning and coordination capacities. In turn, these will ensure that it efficiently allocates national resources to meet the country's developmental needs, especially in the areas of education, health, energy and infrastructure. Democratic development has to be carried out at the same time for democracy to respond to the needs and aspirations of citizens, and for them to own the development outcomes. Democratic participation has to be promoted to give ordinary citizens a voice in the development process.

This book has also laid bare the exclusionary nature of Nigerian politics, which is rigged against a majority of its people, especially women and youths. Nigeria's youth, in particular, must learn from other countries if they want to take over power, or at the very least be relevant in the political space. They will have to first "organise rather than agonise" to use the words of the late iconic pan-Africanist, Tajudeen Abdul-Raheem. They will have to learn to form and run political parties of their own rather than embark on politics of "entryism", that is, joining the political parties of the political class. The current dominant political parties are structured to disempower them. As such, youths will not be allowed to play any meaningful role that will make democracy work for the benefits of all Nigerians.

It is clear from the analysis in this book that the dominant political parties today are not parties of economic and societal transformational change; rather, they are meant to maintain the status quo. It is therefore imperative that the youths organise and mobilise themselves beyond social media, but on the streets, to seek political power. They need to recognise that no class or group cedes power willingly.

Power is won through contests and struggles. It would be naïve for the youths to think that their mere participation in the existing political landscape without a paradigm shift that is rooted on the ideology of development nationalism will lead to structural transformation of the economy and the empowerment of women and youths.

Also, they need to understand that the current political order will not result in an enhancement of human wellbeing. If anything, *entryism* politics by the youths will merely incorporate only a few while it continues to be rigged against a majority of the Nigerian youth and women. Therefore, an important starting point to have a political paradigm shift is for the youths to form political parties of their own. This will simultaneously intensify popular struggles to ensure that the political system and its outcomes incorporate their needs and aspirations, while at the same time holding public officials at all levels – local, state and federal – accountable.

There are ample examples Nigerian youths could learn from. The Economic Freedom Front (EFF) in South Africa led by Julius Malema provides a good example. Expelled with his colleagues from the African National Congress (ANC), Malema and his comrades who were mostly youths formed the EFF in 2013. Not content with political freedom, they focused on economic freedom that will enable South Africans, especially blacks, to live a decent life, be gainfully employed, learn necessary skills, acquire assets and own businesses. To them, while their parents fought against apartheid for political freedom, their generation wants to fight for economic freedom. Since its formation seven years ago, the EFF has played a decisive role in saving South Africa's democracy. Without it, little would have been known about the extent of corruption and state capture in South Africa with its adverse effects on corroding state institutions, democracy and the provision of basic services to ordinary citizens. Through its struggles, some in parliament, the EFF has put the question of land redistribution on the political agenda of South Africa.

Lastly, enhancing the capacity of the Nigerian state requires the digitalisation of the payroll system that captures the biometrics of public servants. This will enhance the organisational capacity of the state and eliminate the problem of ghost workers. It will also save the government precious billions of naira that could be invested in education, healthcare, the provision of a social safety net and the provision of physical infrastructure, including energy, roads and railways. President Buhari has obviously already taken some steps in this regard. In fact, Nigeria should adopt e-governance to enhance the efficiency of the state and to reduce corruption.

All of the above calls for Nigeria to embrace the concept and practice of good development governance, discussed extensively in this book.

Postscript

Nigeria of
My Dream

I dream of a prosperous country where every Nigerian will live in dignity. I dream of an end to high levels of poverty, inequality and unemployment in Nigeria. I dream of a Nigeria where the rule of law will prevail and human rights will be respected.

I dream of a Nigeria where government at all levels will prioritise human capital development, and industrial development. I dream of a country where government will ensure that citizens have access to quality healthcare and where the rich will patronise local hospitals rather than go abroad for medical treatment. I dream of local hospitals that can provide the same quality of healthcare as their counterparts anywhere in the world. I dream of a Nigeria where people die in the presence of loved ones rather than in lonely foreign hospitals. I dream of a Nigeria with vastly reduced infant and maternal mortality rates. I dream of a country where the rich invest in the health sector—build

143

world class hospitals—rather than waste money to place adverts for obituaries of loved ones, most of whom die because of the poor state of Nigerian healthcare.

I dream of a Nigeria where every child has access to quality education: a country with some of the best universities in the world, which parents will see as first choice for their children. I dream of truly world-class research universities in Nigeria. I dream of an era where there will be no strikes by academic and non-academic staff in our higher education institutions. I dream of student unions that will truly prioritise the welfare of students. I dream of an end to cultism on Nigerian campuses. I dream of a Nigeria where lecturers will not seek sexual favours from students, and where lecturers will not take credit for the work of students as their own. I dream of a country where admission to higher education institutions will be on merit.

I dream of a Nigeria where every child, especially the girl child, will have access to quality education at all levels; a country where the girl child is in school rather than being married off; and a society where the girl child has the same rights as the boy child.

I dream of a united, stable and peaceful country. I dream of a Nigeria where ethnic and religious militancy will be a thing of the past, and where there will be no basis to reward ethnic and religious militants with amnesty and government contracts.

I dream of a country where freedom reigns. I dream of a country where citizens will reclaim their humanity. I dream of a Nigeria where citizens will stop worshipping the god of money. I dream of a country where people will worship the creator – the real God and not "the Nigerian god". I dream of a Nigeria where everyone will be defined by the contents of their character rather than their religious and ethnic backgrounds, or by their state of origin. I dream of a country where our common humanity and citizenship define us.

I dream of a Nigeria with a well-equipped police force, where officers do not have to use their personal resources to furnish their offices, and where they do not have to use their own mobile phones to carry out official duties because of government's neglect. I dream of a police force that can protect the lives and property of citizens. I dream of a police force that will serve our people and one whose officers do not solicit or accept bribes. I dream of a country where our navy protects our waters and where the tasks are not outsourced to so-called ex-militants.

I dream of an efficient and effective aviation sector, where there will be no air disasters and no flight delays; where airlines behave with professionalism comparable with world standards. I dream of a society where customers will be queens and kings. I dream of an aviation sector that will be planned for a growing population. I dream of a country that renovates and builds airports for today and tomorrow. I dream of the day when it will take passengers at our international airports less than ten minutes to go through immigration. I dream of a functional rail system and motorable roads, with the resultant decline in road accidents.

I dream of a country where public servants will be servants and not lords over citizens. I dream of a Nigeria governed by decent and patriotic people rather than criminals who parade themselves as politicians. I dream of a country where politics is a second profession; where a politician, who does not win an election, goes back to his or her primary means of livelihood. I dream of a Nigeria where public service is not a means of primitive accumulation and of a society where public officials will not loot the national treasury and our commonwealth. I dream of a Nigeria where those that attempt to dip their hands into the national purse become outcasts in society and are not rewarded with traditional and religious titles.

I dream of a country that rewards hard work and excellence, where entrepreneurs and not politicians are the richest. I dream of a society driven by a politics of ideas rather than godfatherism, and ethnic and religious considerations. I dream of a country where gender equality is practiced in all walks of life, including the political sphere. I dream of development and governance, and consequently public policy, based on scientific ideas; hence, evidence-based facts, rather than myths and superstitions.

I dream of a Nigeria with purposeful leadership that will put national interests above individual and sectional interests. I dream of leaders that will develop the productive capacities of our country, including human capital. I dream of a country with a strong industrial base that will export rather than import finished products. I dream of a country where manufacturing of commercial products and innovations/inventions take place in every corner rather than religious houses sprouting in every street corner. I dream of a post-oil Nigeria where the manufacturing and high value-added service sectors contribute more to exports, employment and GDP.

I dream of a Nigeria with leaders like Lee Kuan Yew, who will transform our economy from primary sector dependence to high value-added manufacturing and a high service sector base. I dream of a president who will inspire Nigerians to actualise their human potential. I dream of a Nigerian president that is not defined by region, ethnicity or religion.

I dream of a Nigeria with moral icons like Nelson Mandela and Desmond Tutu. I dream of a day Nigerians will have leaders that are unifying figures and who command moral authority. I dream of a country with true statesmen/women.

I dream of the day when every Nigerian will experience uninterrupted power supply. I dream of a country that will take advantage of our natural environment to generate electricity. I dream of green energy as one of the main sources of power supply in Nigeria. I dream of a Nigeria where oil companies will observe the international standards of environmental protection.

Nigeria: Democracy without Development. How to fix it

146

I dream of a Nigeria with free and fair elections, where politicians will not be experts in writing election results to change the will of the people. I dream of the day when genuine losers of elections will accept the results and move on until the next election. I dream of a Nigeria without electoral thuggery. I dream of a country where our best, both morally and professionally, will dominate the political space. I dream of a Nigeria where election periods will not be cycles of politically motivated killings.

I dream of a Nigeria inspiring the African continent and the black race to become important players in the international community. I dream of Nigerians heading major international development bodies like the World Bank and the African Development Bank, not because of acts of charity, but because of the strength of its economy.

I dream, I dream, and I dream of a better Nigeria. I dream of a brighter future for our children. I dream that all Nigerians work to make these dreams a reality.

Acknowledgments

My interest in the political economy of development is informed by the need to contribute to the development of Nigeria, the country of my birth, South Africa my adopted home, and Africa in general. To be able to meaningfully contribute to the development of my continent requires that I understand economic theories and the methodologies in which they are based. I gravitated towards comparative political economy as a response to the erroneous, yet dominant scholarly work and policies on the role of the state in development. My work, both in academia and policy-making, has consequently been informed by the developmental state as a theory of development. I always marvelled at how countries like South Korea and Malaysia which Nigeria was at par with in the early 1970s have transformed to developed economies whilst Nigeria has remained underdeveloped. The story of the divergent trajectories of Nigeria and Malaysia is starkly illustrated by the following example: In the 1960s, Nigeria exported palm seedlings to Malaysia. Today, Malaysia has not only mechanised the cultivation of its palm plantations but has also ensured that it is a leading global player in the palm production and exportation (including expertise and human capital) value chain. One need not ponder too hard to understand how they have become a upper middle income economy. In contrast, Nigeria has remained a lower middle income developing country, with too few palm plantations to employ the amount of labour necessary to stem the increase of its ever growing army of jobless or underemployed youth or export the produce in significant quantities to earn badly needed foreign exchange to shore up its economy against the vagaries of crude oil dependence. Resolving this puzzle preoccupied me but I never thought it would culminate in my writing a book on Nigeria now. I was working on a book about democracy and development in Africa when I was encouraged to first write a book with the same theme on Nigeria. My thanks will therefore go first to Innocent Chukwuma and Professor Adebayo Olukoshi for planting the seeds of writing this book in my mind.

A number of scholars have played important roles in shaping my intellectual views, Professors Jonathon Moses, Peter Evans, Thandika Mkandawire and Linda Weiss are a few of them. I am especially indebted to Professor Moses who read and commented on every draft of this book.

Special thanks go to my friend and brother (and now my boss), Mallam Nasir Ahmad El-Rufai, who through a chance encounter in Tokyo in 2008 encouraged me to return to Nigeria to work with him and other like-minded Nigerians to contribute to the development of the country. I am glad I took his advice and returned home when I did. My return to the country and engagement in the political process have given me greater insights into the Nigerian democratic experience and development challenges. Since my return, Mallam El-Rufai and his family have embraced me as one of their own. Because of them, Kaduna has now become my home and I am happily learning to speak Hausa to make this process of settling easier. I am very grateful to the

El-Rufai family for their love and support. I must acknowledge also those friends I met through Governor El-Rufai. Many of them have become important sounding boards in my professional life.

I owe a huge debt of gratitude to Idris Othman. He constantly checks in with me to find out how I am doing. Idris doesn't leave me room to doubt that he is rooting for me and wants me to win. Hadiza Bala Usman, A. U. Mustapha, S.A.N, Martin Akumazi, Gambo Hamza and Tijanni Abdullahi are worth mentioning for their constant encouragement and nuggets of wisdom. I am profoundly grateful to Thamos Gyang for his wise counsel and friendship, and to Safiya Umar, a true sister, whose home is open to me at any time of the day. You both have enriched my life in so many ways.

It would be remiss of me not to thank one of Nigeria's most accomplished political economists and public intellectuals, Professor Pat Utomi, who encouraged me to bring my knowledge and experience to bear on the Nigerian political and development process. My friend, Dr Otive Igbuzor, has been a pillar of support in several ways. His commitment to the Nigerian project and admonition that we all must engage in nation-building not just in words but in deeds, is something that I take to heart. Thank you Otive. Conversations with my friend, Tanimu Yakubu, vastly enriched my knowledge of Nigeria's political economy. Also worthy of mention is my late friend, an outstanding scholar, activist, pan Africanist and humanist, Professor Abubukar Momoh with whom I had numerous conversations that gave me a better understanding of the Nigerian political economy.

I must also extend my profound gratitude to Professors Jibril Ibrahim, Ayokunu Adedokun and Dr Sam Amadi for their comments which added great value to this book.

Over the years, I have been privileged to engage and work with a number of people who have shaped my political and intellectual views. These include former South African Minister of Home Affairs, Malusi Gigaba, Minister Thoko Didiza, Duma Gqubule, Mondli Makhanya,

Professor Richard Levin, Professor Chris Malikane, Joel Netshitenzhe, Professor Alan Hirsch, Langa Zitha, Dr Temba Masilela, Dr Charles Hangoro and Febe Potgieter-Gqubule. Some of them are already urging me to write a sequel to my first book on the democratic developmental state in South Africa. All in good time! I owe special gratitude to Jeremy Cronin, the former Deputy General Secretary of the South African Communist Party and Deputy Minister of Public Works, for his guidance on how to navigate the South African political arena and for his solidarity with the Nigerian pro-democracy movement in the 1990s, as well as for both the stimulating political and intellectual discussions. Over time, our relationship has evolved and we have become kindred spirits. The gift of Jeremy's friendship is one that I dearly cherished. I have also benefited immensely from innumerable discussions with many academics, policy-makers and development activists in and outside the African continent, who are too numerous to mention. They know themselves and I want to use this opportunity to convey my gratitude to them.

I am proud to call the following people my friends: Dr Felix Woke, Professor Ola Busari, Dr Sam Agbo, Dr Ken Uche Kalunta, Dr. Okwudile Akarue, Dr Nkem Khumbah, Dr Aloy Chife, Professor Harrisson Atangana, Mahmud Abdul, Wole Olaleye and Nolwazi Gasa. The camaraderie we share has been a tremendous source of strength in my private and professional life and I thank them all immensely for it.

In Nigeria, three young men inspire me with their patriotism, hard work and dedication to the development of Nigeria. They are Japheth Omojuwa, Bello El-Rufai and Hafiz Bayero. Japheth in particular, gave me invaluable advice without which this book may not have seen the light of day. Thank you all so much.

Thanks are also due to Peter Jones, Umar Farouq Saleh, Joel Adeoga, Saude Amina Atoyebi and Momoh Adejoh for the great resource they are. I also appreciate Dr Salisu Suleiman and Muhammad Sani Abdullahi, two amiable scholars with vast experience in Nigeria's development.

I thank the West African Regional Office of the Ford Foundation for providing grants for the initial research and publication of this book. I am also heavily indebted to the National Bureau of Statistics (NBS) under the able leadership of Dr Yemi Kale for providing me with a lot of the development data critical to the veracity of the propositions put forward in this book. I do hope policy-makers will better utilise the data provided by the NBS in public policy making. Over the course of many interviews, Steve Oronsaye, Dr Joe Abah and a host of other interviewees, shared their experiences and knowledge of the Nigerian civil service with me. I really do appreciate them and the wealth of information their interviews provided.

My acknowledgments would be incomplete if I didn't mention my publisher, Emilia Asim-Ita and her team at A'Lime Media Limited for their dedication to this project and bringing this dream to fruition. I know I can be a hard task master but they dealt with all my concerns like the true professionals they are. I am grateful to Eikon Grae for the cover design. I love it.

Sincere appreciation is due to my siblings, especially Janet Edigheji and Vincent Edigheji for their love and encouragement.

Most importantly, I owe this book to the Nigerian people. This book is yours and I did not want to take it with me to the cemetery when I die. It is therefore a book written as part of the project to "Die Empty" to quote Dr. Myles Munroe. Finally, the analysis and conclusions in this book are mine alone, as a scholar and development expert, and not of anyone or the government I currently work for.

References

Abati, Reuben. 2018. "Understanding APC and the Crisis of Defections". *Premium Times*. August 3, 2018. https://opinion.premiumtimesng.com/2018/08/03/understanding-apc-and-the-crisis-of-defections-by-reuben-abati/ (Accessed on August 3, 2018).

Abdul, Mahmud. 2013. "The June 12, 1993 Struggles: A Personal Account". *The Scoop*. June 12, 2013. http://www.thescoopng.com/2013/06/12/abdul-mahmud-the-june-12-1993-struggles-a-personal-account/ (Accessed on June 12, 2013).

Abrahamsen, Rita. 2001. "Democratisation–Part of the Problem or the Solution to Africa's 'Failed States." (Unpublished thesis). University of Wales.

Abrahamsen, Rita. 2000. *Disciplining democracy: Development Discourse and Good Governance in Africa*. London and New York: Zed Books.

Acemoglu, Daron and Robinson, James A. 2012. *Why Nations Fail: The Origins of Power, Prosperity and Poverty*. London: Profile Books Ltd.

Adeosun, Kemi. 2018a. "19m tax payers: Fed Govt to mobilize more revenues- Adeosun." http://thenationonlineng.net/19m-tax-payers-fed-govt-to-mobilize-more-revenues-adeosun/amp/?__twitter_impression=true (Accessed on November 20, 2019)

Adeosun, Kemi. 2018b. Tweet on February 20, 2018. https://twitter.com/HMKemiAdeosun. @HMKemiAdeosun

Adesina, Akin. 2018. "GDP growth is not enough. Growth must be felt in the lives of people. Nobody eats GDP". "Twitter / @Akin_adesina. January 25, 2018, 5.01p.m., https://twitter.com/akin_adesina/status/956557748925280256?lang=en. (Accessed on January 27, 2018).

African Development Bank. 2011a. "Market Brief –The Middle of the Pyramid: Dynamics of the Middle Class in Africa." (*AfDB. Chief Economist Complex*). April 20. https://www.afdb.org/en/documents/document/market-brief-the-middle-of-the-pyramid-dynamics-of-the-middle-class-in-africa-23582. (Accessed on April 2, 2018).

African Development Bank. 2011b. "Enhancing Capacity for Youth Development in Africa. Some Emerging Lessons." (*AfDB Chief Economist Complex*. 2). December 21. https://www.afdb.org/fileadmin/uploads/afdb/Documents/Publications/Africa%20Capacity%20Dev%20Brief_Africa%20Capacity%20Dev%20Brief.pdf. (Accessed on December 9, 2017)

African Development Bank, OECD and UNDP. 2015. "African Economic Outlook: Regional Development and Spatial Inclusion." May 25. https://www.afdb.org/fileadmin/uploads/afdb/Documents/Publications/AEO2015_EN.pdf (Accessed on December 20, 2017).

African Union Commission. 2004. "African Charter on Democracy, Elections and Governance." https://au.int/en/treaties/african-charter-democracy-elections-and-governance (Accessed on May 20, 2019).

African Union and United Nations Economic Commission for Africa. 2012. "Illicit Financial Flows: Report of the High Level Panel on Illicit Financial Flows from Africa." December 9. http://www.uneca.org/sites/default/files/PublicationFiles/iff_main_report_26feb_en.pdf. (Accessed on December 10, 2016).

Akinduro, Olufunto, and Masterson, Grant. 2018. "Encoding the Rules: Capturing the State Through Electoral Process." In *State Capture in Africa: Old Threats, New Packages?*, ed. Melanie Meiroti and Grant Masterson. Johannesburg: Electoral Institute for Sustainable Democracy in Africa, (59 -70).

Alfonso, Haroldo D. 1997. "Political Decentralization and Popular Alternatives: A View from the South." In Michael Kautman and Haroldo Dilla Alfonso, *eds. Community Power for Grassroots Democracy: The Transformation of Social Life*. London and New Jersey: Zed Books, (170 - 188).

Amnesty International. 2014. *Injustice Incorporated: Corporate Abuses and the Human Rights Remedy*. London: Amnesty International Ltd.

Annan, Kofi. 2016. "Africa and the Global Security Architecture." April 16. http://www.kofiannanfoundation.org/speeches/africa-global-security-architecture/ (Accessed on April 16, 2017).

Annan, Kofi. 1999. "In The State of the World's Children Education." December 12. https://www.unicef.org/sowc99/sowc99a.pdf (Accessed on December 12, 2019).

Atuobi, Samuel M. 2008. "Election-Related Violence in Africa." https://www.academia.edu/22759489/Election_Related_Violence_in _Africa. (Accessed on November 10, 2016).

Awa, Eme. 1991. "Democracy and Governance in Africa: Preliminary Statement". In Aderinwale, A and Mosha, F. G. N. eds. *Democracy and Governance in Africa: Conclusions and Papers presented at a conference of the Africa leadership Forum* on November 29, 1991 at Ota, Ogun State, Nigeria.

Ayodele, Elijah O. 2011. "Abandonment of Construction Projects in Nigeria: Causes and Effects." *Journal of Emerging Trends in Economics and Management Sciences*, 2 (April): (142–145).

Babalola, Afe. 2018. "Political Party Finance and Godfatherism." *Vanguard Newspaper.* May 23. https://www.vanguardngr.com/2018/05/political-party-finance-godfatherism/ (Accessed on March 12, 2019).

Banke-Thomas, Adura. 2015. "The Emigration of Doctors from Nigeria is not Today's Problem, it is Tomorrow's." October 15. https://blogs.lse.ac.uk/africaatlse/2018/10/15/the-emigration-of-doctors-from-nigeria-is-not-todays-problem-it-is-tomorrows/ (Accessed on May 5, 2016).

BBC. 2019. "Nigeria Election 2019: How Godfathers Influence Politics." February 4. https://www.bbc.com/news/world-africa-47089372 (Accessed on April 3, 2019).

Blavatnik School of Government and the Institute for Government. 2017. *The International Civil Service Effectiveness Index.* Oxford: Oxford University.

Boix, Carles. 2003. *Democracy and Redistribution*. Cambridge: Cambridge University Press.

Breslin, Shaun G. 1996. "China: Developmental State or Dysfunctional Development?" *Third World Quarterly*, 17(4): (689–706).

Buhari, Muhammadu. 2019a. "Address at the Formal Acceptance of the Report of the Committee to Access Impact and Readiness for the Africa Continental Free Trade Area Agreement (AfCFTA)." June 27. https://statehouse.gov.ng/news/afcfta-president-buhari-approves-establishment-of-national-action-committee-nac/ (Accessed on June 27, 2019).

Buhari, Muhammadu. 2019b. "President Buhari Reveals How He'll Fight Corruption in Second Term." *Daily Post*. June 11. https://dailypost.ng/2019/06/11/june-12-president-buhari-reveals-hell-fight-corruption-second-term-full-text/. (Accessed on December 10, 2019).

Buhari, Mohammadu. 2018. "Speech by His Excellency, Muhammadu Buhari, President of the Federal Republic of Nigeria, at the signing into law, the 2018 Appropriation Bill." President Villa, Abuja. June 20. https://punchng.com/president-buharis-speech-at-the-signing-of-2018-budget-into-law/ (Accessed on June 20, 2019).

Buhari, Mohammadu. 2016. "President Buhari's Democracy Day message to Nigerians". May 29.

Centre for Democracy and Development. 2019. "Nigeria Electoral Trends". https://www.academia.edu/38572951/Nigeria_Electoral_Trends (Accessed on January 3, 2020).

Channel TV. 2019. "During Your First Tenure I Didn't Get Employment Letter For My Constituents," - Senator Tinubu Tells Fashola. 29 July, 2019. https://www.channelstv.com/2019/07/29/during-your-first-tenure-i-didnt-get-employment-letter-for-my-constituents-senator-tinubu-tells-fashola/ (Accessed on July 29, 2019).

Chukwuemeka, Emma; Oji, Richard and Chukwurah, Daniel J. 2017. "Give Them their Rights: A Critical Review of Godfather and of Grandson Politics in Nigeria." April 2017. https://www.longdom.org/open-access/give-them-their-rights-a-critical-review-of-godfather-and-godson-politics-in-nigeria-2315-7844-1-133.pdf (Accessed on December 10, 2019).

Daily Post (2018) "Delta government weeds out 26, 000 ghost workers in public service, 18, 000 others with fake certificates". https://dailypost.ng/2018/04/17/delta-govt-weeds-26-000-ghost-workers-public-service-18-000-others-fake-certificates/ (Accessed on April 18, 2018).

Daily Trust. 2019. "Are Godfathers Too Powerful in Nigerian Politics?" *Daily Trust.* June 1,. https://www.dailytrust.com.ng/are-godfathers-too-powerful-in-nigerian-politics.html (Accessed on June 2, 2019).

Daily Trust. 2018. "Politicians Must Care for Nigerians, not just their Allowances – Cardinal Onaiyekan." *Daily Trust.* November 25. https://www.dailytrust.com.ng/politicians-must-care-for-nigerians-not-just-their-allowances-cardinal-onaiyekan.html. (Accessed on June 2, 2019).

Dangote, Aliko. 2019. "Nigeria Struggling With Electricity Supply For 18 Years To Add 1,000 Megawatts" *SaharaReporters.* June 9, 2019. http://saharareporters.com/2019/06/09/nigeria-struggling-electricity-supply-18-years-add-1000-megawatts-%E2%80%93dangote. (Accessed on June 10, 2019).

Deyo, Fredric. 1987. "Introduction." In Fredric C. D, *ed. The Political Economy of New Asian Industrialism*. Ithaca and London: Cornell University Press. pp. (203–226).

Economic Intelligence Unit. 2019. "Democracy Index." March 23. https://www.eiu.com/topic/democracy-index (Accessed on March 23, 2019).

Edigheji, Omano. 2013. "National Long-Term Visions and Development Plans of African Countries: A Critical Review of Their Gender Content." The African Institute for Economic Development and Planning (IDEP).

Edigheji, Omano. 2010. "Constructing a Democratic Developmental State in South Africa: The Potentials and Challenges." In Omano Edigheji, ed. Constructing *a Democratic Developmental State in South Africa: The Potentials and Challenges*. Cape Town: HSRC Press. (1- 33).

Edigheji, Omano. 2007. "The State, State-Society Relations and Developing Countries' Economic Performance." PhD Thesis. Trondheim: Norwegian University of Science and Technology.

Edigheji, Omano. 2006. "Political Representation in Africa: Towards a Conceptual Framework." *African Development,* XXXI (August) (3): (99-119).

Edigheji, Omano. 2005. *A Democratic Developmental State in Africa?* Johannesburg: Centre for Policy Studies *(*Research Report). (105 -127)

Edigheji, Omano; El-Rufai, Nasir; Busari, Ola and Moses, Jonathon. 2013. "In the National Interest: A Critical Review of the Petroleum Industry Bill 2012." *Policy Review No. 1.* July. Abuja: Centre for Africa's Progress and Prosperity.

El-Rufai, Nasir, A. 2013. *The Accidental Public Servant.* Ibadan: Safari Books Ltd.

El-Rufai, Nasir, A. 2010. "Emerging Leaders". *Sahara Reporters,* October 17. http://saharareporters.com/2010/10/17/emerging-leaders-nasir-ahmad-el-rufai (Accessed on July 8, 2017).

European Union Election Observation Mission. 2019. "EU Election Observation Mission: Nigeria General Elections 2019. Final Report". February 25. https://eeas.europa.eu/sites/eeas/files/nigeria_2019_eu_eom_final_re port-web.pdf (Accessed on November 10, 2019).

Evans, Peter. 2010. "Constructing the 21st Century Developmental State: Potentialities and Pitfalls". In Omano Edigheji, ed. *Constructing a Democratic Developmental State in South Africa: The Potentials and Challenges..* Cape Town: HSRC Press.

Evans, Peter. 1995. *Embedded Autonomy: States and Industrial Transformation.* Princeton, NJ: Princeton University Press.

Evans, Peter and Rauch, James. 1999. "Bureaucracy and Growth: A Cross-national Analysis of the Effects of Weberian State Structures on Economic Growth." *American Sociological Review,* (May) 64(5): (748–765).

Food and Agriculture Organization (FAO). 2019. "The State of Food Security and Nutrition in the World 2019: Safeguarding Against Economic Slowdowns and Downturns." July 15.

http://www.fao.org/3/ca5162en/ca5162en.pdf (Accessed on November 12, 2019).

Food and Agriculture Organization (FAO) 2017. "The State of Food Security and Nutrition in the World 2017. Building Resilience for Peace and Food Security." September 13. http://www.fao.org/3/a-I7695e.pdf (Accessed on December 10, 2019).

Fika, Adamu. 2014. "Evolution of the Public Service in Nigeria." Paper presented at the 60th Anniversary Celebration of the Establishment of the Public Service Commission, FCT, Abuja, March 31, 2014.

Fukuyama, Francis. 2012. "Why Public Administration Gets No Respect But Should". *The American Interest*. January 1. https://www.the-american-interest.com/2012/01/01/why-public-administration-gets-no-respect-but-should/ (Accessed on December 21, 2018).

Gills, Barry K. 2000. "Introduction: Globalization and the Politics of Resistance". In *Gills B.K, eds. Globalization and the Politics of Resistance.*, New York: Palgrave.

Human Rights Watch. 2007a. "Corruption, Godfatherism and the Funding of Political Violence in Nigeria." August 15. https://www.hrw.org/reports/nigeria1007/5.htm (Accessed on January 4, 2014).

Human Rights Watch. 2007b. "Godfatherism in Anambra State." February 12.. https://www.hrw.org/reports/2007/nigeria1007/5.htm (Accessed on January 4, 2019).

Ibekwe, Nicholas. 2016. "CBN Recruitment Scandal: Job Titles for Buhari, Ministers' Relatives Released." *Premium Times*. March 30. http://www.premiumtimesng.com/news/top-news/201055-cbn-recruitment-scandal-job-titles-buhari-ministers-relatives-released.html (Accessed on October 10, 2019).

Ibrahim, Jibril. 2019. "Mass Killings, Atrocities and Scorched Earth in Nigeria: Tracing The Trajectory." *Newsdairy Online*. April 11. https://newsdiaryonline.com/mass-killings-atrocities-and-scorched-earth-in-nigeria-tracing-the-trajectory-by-jibrin-ibrahim/ (Accessed on June 17, 2019).

Igbokwe, Joe. 1999. *Heroes of Democracy*. Lagos: Clear Vision Limited.

Igbuzor, Otive and Edigheji, Omano. 2003. "Constitutions, Electoral Process and the Future of Democratic Governance in Africa". Paper presented at the African Conference on Elections, Democracy and Governance, Pretoria, South Africa, April 7–10, 2003.

IndexMundi. 2018a. "Nigeria – Life Expectancy at Birth." https://www.indexmundi.com/g/r.aspx?c=ni&v=30. (Accessed on October 7, 2018).

IndexMundi. 2018b. "Physicians per 100,000 People." https://www.indexmundi.com/facts/indicators/SH.MED.PHYS.ZS (Accessed on May 5, 2019).

International Crisis Group. 2018. "Stopping Nigeria's Spiralling Farmer-Herder Violence." August 8. *https://www.crisisgroup.org/africa/west-africa/nigeria/262-stopping-nigerias-spiralling-farmer-herder-violence*. (Accessed on November 10, 2019).

International Labour Office. 2015. "Towards Inclusive and Sustainable Development in Africa Through Decent Work." Paper presented at the 13ᵗʰ Regional Meeting, November 30–3 December. Addis Ababa, Ethiopia.

Jega, Attahiru. 2001. "Democracy in Nigeria: Concepts, Representations and Expectations" In Daniel C Bach, Yann Lebeau. and Kunle Amuwo, eds. *The Abacha Years (1993 – 1998)*, Ibadan: French Institute for Research in Africa.

John, Elnathan. 2012. "How to Worship the Nigerian god". *Daily Post*. August 21. https://dailypost.ng/2012/08/21/elnathan-john-how-worship-nigerian-god/ (Accessed on September 12, 2018).

Johnson, Chalmers. 1987. "Political Institutions and Economic Performance: The Government-Business Relationship in Japan, South Korea and Taiwan." In Fredric C. Deyo. ed. The *Political Economy of New Asian Industrialism*. Ithaca and London: Cornell University Press, pp. (136–164).

Johnson, Chalmers. 1982. *MITI and the Japanese Miracle: The Growth of Industrial Policy, 1925-1975*. Stanford: Stanford University Press.

Kapoor, Kapil; Mansaray, Hasaantu; Sennet, Laura and Pitt, Oscar. 2019. "Fourth Industrial Revolution Jobs, and Skills." In Celestin Monga, Abebe Shimeles, and Andinet Woldemichael, eds. *Creating Decent Jobs: Strategies, Policies, and Instruments*. Abidjan: African Development Bank. (29 - 48)

Kaufmann, Daniel; Kraay, Aart and Mastruzzi, Massimo. 2009. "Governance Matters VIII: Aggregate and Individual Governance Indicators, 1996-2008." Policy Research working paper; no. WPS 4978. Washington, DC: World Bank.

http://documents.worldbank.org/curated/en/598851468149673121/
Governance-matters-VIII-aggregate-and-individual-governance-
indicators-1996-2008 (Accessed on December 10, 2019).

Keeley, Brian. 2016. "What About Africa". June 15.
https://knowledgeresources.wordpress.com/2016/04/11/what-about-
africa/ (Accessed on July 24, 2017).

Kharas, Home; Kristofer, Hamel and Hofer, Martin. 2018. "The
Start of a New Poverty Narrative." June 19.
https://www.brookings.edu/blog/future-
development/2018/06/19/the-start-of-a-new-poverty-narrative/
(Accessed on June 26, 2018).

Kim, Eun Mee. 2010. "Limits of The Authoritarian Developmental
State of South Korea." In Omano Edigheji, ed. *Constructing a
Democratic Developmental State in South Africa: The Potentials
and Challenges*. Cape Town: HSRC Press.

Kingibe, Babagana. 2013. "The Public Service in a Constitutional
Democracy: the Nigerian Experience." Public Lecture presented at
the Mohammed Lawal Uwais Public Service Award Lectures, FCT,
September 11. Abuja.

Kohli, Atul. 2010. "State Capacity for Development." Public
Lecture presented at the Human Sciences Research Council, May
11. Pretoria, South Africa.

Laakso, Liisa and Olukoshi, Adebayo. 1996. "The Crisis of the
Post-Colonial Nation-State Project in Africa." In Liisa Laakso and
Adebayo Olukoshi, eds. *Challenges to the Nation-State in Africa*.
Uppsala: Nordiska Afrkaninstitutet. (33 – 45)

Leftwich, Adrian. 2010. "Beyond Institutions: Rethinking the Role of Leaders, Elites and Coalitions in the Institutional Formation of Developmental States and Strategies." *Forum for Development Studies* 37(1): (93–111).

Lin, Justin Y. and Monga, Celestin. 2010. "Growth Identification and Facilitation: the Role of the State in the Dynamics of Structural Change." Policy Research Working Paper 5313. Washington, DC: World Bank. June 7.

Lodge, Tom. 2018. "State Capture: Conceptual Considerations." In Melanie Meiroti, and Grant Masterson, eds. *State Capture in Africa: Old Threats, New Packages?* Johannesburg: Electoral Institute for Sustainable Democracy in Africa. (13 -28)

Logan, Carolyn and Penar, Peter. 2019. "Are Africans' Freedoms Slipping Away?" Afrobarometer Policy Paper No. 55. April. http://afrobarometer.org/sites/default/files/publications/Policy%20p apers/ab_r7_policypaperno55_are_freedoms_slipping_away_in_afri ca_1.pdf (Accessed on May 25, 2019).

Little, Daniel. 2003. *The Paradox of Wealth and Poverty: Mapping the Ethical Dilemmas of Global Development.* Colorado: Westview Press.

Maboloc, Christopher R. 2018. "Democracy and a Can of Corned Beef". *Inquirer.* December 29. http://opinion.inquirer.net/109841/democracy-can-corned-beef/amp?__twitter_impression=true (Accessed on January 19, 2019).

Mann, Michael. 2003. "The Autonomous Power of the State: Its Origins, Mechanisms and Results." In Neil Brenner., Bob Jessop., Martin Jones, and Gordon Macleod, eds. *State/Space: A Reader*

Oxford: Blackwell Publishing, (185 -213)

Mandela, Nelson. 1998. "Welcome Address" Presented at the 53rd United Nations General Assembly. New York, USA. 21 September 21.

Matlosa, Khabele. 2019. "Facebook post by David Omozuafoh." June 14, 2019 at 12:49p.m. https://facebook.com/10000162826071/posts/2393877187343200/ (Accessed on June 16, 2019).

Matlosa, Khabele; Prah, Kwesi K; Chiroro, Bertha and Toulou, L. 2008. "Introduction." In K. Matlosa, K. Prah, B. Chiroro, and L. Toulou, eds. *The State, Democracy and Poverty Eradication in Africa*. Johannesburg: Electoral Institute of Southern Africa. (1-11)

Mba, David. 2018. "Unschooled and Underfunded: How Nigeria's Desperately Failing its Young." *African Arguments*. August 6. http://africanarguments.org/2018/08/06/unschooled-underfunded-nigeria-schools-failing-young/ (Accessed on August 7, 2019).

McKinsey and Company. 2010. "Africa's Path to Growth: Sector by Sector." June 7. http://www.mckinsey.com/global-themes/middle-east-and-africa/africas-path-to-growth-sector-by-sector(Accessed on December 10, 2017).

Mhone, Guy. 2003. "Democratisation, Economic Liberalisation and the Quest for Sustainable Development in South Africa." In Guy Mhone and Omano Edigheji, eds. *Governance in the new South Africa: The Challenges of Globalisation*. Cape Town. University of Cape Town Press. (18 -68)

Mhone, Guy and Edigheji, Omano. 2003. "Towards Developmentalism and Democratic Governance in South Africa." In

Guy Mhone and Omano Edigheji, eds. *Governance in the New South Africa: The Challenges of Globalisation.* Cape Town: University of Cape Town Press. (348 -353)

Mkandawire, Thandika. 1995. "Beyond Crisis: Towards Democratic Developmental States in Africa." Paper Presented at the 8th General Assembly of the Council of the Development of Social Sciences in Africa (CODESRIA), Dakar.

Mkandawire, Thandika. 1992. "Crisis Management and the Making of Choiceless Democracies." In Richard Joseph, *ed. State, Conflict and Democracy in Africa.,* Colorado and London: Rienner Publishers Inc.,

Mohammed, bin Rashid Al Maktoum. 2012. *My Vision: Challenges in the Race for Excellence.* Dubai: Motivate Publishing.

Monga, Celestin. 2019. "Jobs: An African Manifesto." In Celestin Monga., Abebe Shimeles., and Andinet Woldemichael, eds. *Creating Decent Jobs: Strategies, Policies, and Instruments.* Abidjan: African Development Bank.

Mosca, Gaetano. 1896. *The Ruling Class.* New York: McGraw Hill.

Moses, Jonathon. 2010. "Foiling the Resource Curse: Wealth, Equality, Oil and The Norwegian State." In Omano Edigheji, ed. *Constructing a Democratic Developmental State in South Africa: The Potentials and Challenges.* Cape Town: HSRC Press.

Murisa, Tendai. 2015a. "Not Yet Uhuru: Zimbabwe's Halting Attempts at Democracy." In Tendai Murisa and Tendai Chikweche, eds. *Beyond the Crises: Zimbabwe's Prospects for Transformation.* Senegal and Zimbabwe: TrustAfrica. (1 -29)

Murisa, Tendai. 2015b. "The Democracy Manifesto for Zimbabwe." In Tendai Murisa and Tendai Chikweche, eds. *Beyond the Crises: Zimbabwe's Prospects for Transformation.* , Senegal and Zimbabwe: TrustAfrica

National Bureau of Statistics. 2018. *Labour Force Statistics Vol. 2: Employment by Sector Report-Q03 2017.* January. Abuja: NBS.

National Bureau of Statistics. 2017a. *Unemployment/Underemployment Report- Q03 2016. -June.* Abuja: NBS.

National Bureau of Statistics. 2017b. *Labour Force Statistics. Vol. 1. Unemployment and underemployment report Q1 – Q3.* December. Abuja: NBS.

National Bureau of Statistics. 2014. *National Gross Domestic Report -First Quarter.* Abuja: NBS.

North, Douglass. C. 1990. *Institutions, Institutional Change and Economic Performance.* Cambridge: Cambridge University Press.

Numbeo. 2019. "Crime Index for Country 2019 Mid-Year." July 5. https://www.numbeo.com/crime/rankings_by_country.jsp (Accessed on July 6, 2019).

Obama, Barack. 2018. "Transcript: Obama's Speech at the 2018 Nelson Mandela Annual Lecture." July 17. https://www.npr.org/2018/07/17/629862434/transcript-obamas-speech-at-the-2018-nelson-mandela-annual-lecture (Accessed on July 18, 2019).

Obaseki, Godwin. 2019. "Edo Crisis: I Refused to Share State Money with Godfathers Is My Offence." July 20.

https://mail.reubenabati.com.ng/index.php/component/k2/item/7281
-edo-crisis-i-refused-to-share-state-money-with-godfathers-was-my-
offence-obaseki (Accessed on December 20, 2019).

Okeshola, Folashade. 2011. "Violence and Insecurity in Nigeria:
The Bane of National Development." *European Scientific Journal*. 7
(26): (148–156).

Okonjo-Iweala, Ngozi. 2016. "Six Questions African Policymakers
Must Answer Now." March 14.
http://www.cgdev.org/sites/default/files/ngozi-okonjo-oweala-six-
questions.pdf (Accessed on October 2, 2019).

Olukoshi, Adebayo. 2011. *Democratic Governance and
Accountability in Africa: In Search of a Workable Framework.*
Uppsala: Nordiska Afrikan Institutet.

Olukoshi, Adebayo. 1998. *The Elusive Prince of Denmark:
Structural Adjustment and the Crisis of Governance in Africa.*
Uppsala: Nordiska Afrikaninstitutet.

Olukoshi, Adebayo. 1997. "The Left and the Struggle for
Democracy." In Jibrin Ibrahim, eds. *Expanding Democratic Space
in Nigeria.* Dakar: Codesria.

Omojuwa, Joshua J. 2019. *Digital: The new code of wealth – New
opportunities for wealth creation and change.* Lagos: A'Lime Media
Ltd.

Onaiyekan, John. 2019a. "Cardinal Onaiyekan Speaks on who
Nigerians Should Vote for" December 4.
https://www.naijanews.com/2018/12/04/2019-cardinal-onaiyekan-
speaks-on-who-nigerians-should-vote-for (Accessed on June 5,
2019).

Onaiyekan, John. 2019b. "What Archbishop Onaiyekan said about Nigeria's Governorship, State Assembly Elections". *DailyPost*, March 12. https://dailypost.ng/2019/03/12/archbishop-onaiyekan-said-nigerias-governorship-state-assembly-elections/ (Accessed on June 5, 2019).

Onaiyekan, John. 2019c. "Onaiyekan To Politicians: Bad Elections Can't Lead to Good Governance". *Vanguard Newspaper*. March 12. https://www.vanguardngr.com/2019/03/onaiyekan-to-politicians-bad-elections-cant-lead-to-good-governance/ (Accessed on June 5, 2019).

Onaiyekan, John. 2018. "No Credible Presidential Candidate for Nigerians". *Daily Trust*. December 4. https://www.dailytrust.com.ng/2019-no-credible-presidential-candidate-yet-for-nigerians-onaiyekan.html (Accessed on June 5, 2019).

Ostrom, Elinor. 1986. "An Agenda for the Study of Institutions." *Public Choice*. (48): (3–25).

Ostry, Jonathan D; Loungani, Prakash and Furceri, David. 2016. "Neoliberalism: Oversold?" *Finance and Development*. June 53 (2).

Oxfam. 2017. *Inequality in Nigeria: Exploring the Drivers*. September 2017. https://d1tn3vj7xz9fdh.cloudfront.net/s3fs-public/file_attachments/cr-inequality-in-nigeria-170517-en.pdf. (Accessed on June 9, 2019).

Page, John. 2015. "Meeting Africa's Aspirations: The Sustainable Development Goals in 2016." In Sy Amadou, *ed. Foresight Africa: Top Priorities for Africa in 2016.*. Africa Growth Initiatives at Brookings.

Pew Research Center. 2018. "The World's Most Committed Christians live in Africa, Latin America – and the U.S". August 22. https://www.pewresearch.org/fact-tank/2018/08/22/the-worlds-most-committed-christians-live-in-africa-latin-america-and-the-u-s/ (Accessed on September 13, 2019).

Pires, Roberto; Rocha, Cristina and Alexandre de Avila Gomide. 2014. "State Capacities, Democracy, and Development Projects in Contemporary Brazil." Paper Presented at RC37 283, the 3rd International Political Science Association World Congress, July 19–24. Montreal, Canada.

Premium Times. 2019a. "Why Supreme Court ruled against APC in Zamfara" May 24. https://www.premiumtimesng.com/news/headlines/331517-why-supreme-court-ruled-against-apc-in-zamfara.html (Accessed on May 25, 2019).

Premium Times. 2019b. "It's Official: Nigeria Gravely Lacks Doctors to Address Citizens' Health Needs". February 4. https://www.premiumtimesng.com/health/health-investigations/309633-its-official-nigeria-gravely-lacks-doctors- to-address-citizens-health-needs.html (Accessed on June 18, 2019).

Premium Times. 2018. "Bayelsa Discovers 28,000 Ghost Workers." June 28. https://www.premiumtimesng.com/regional/south-south-regional/274207-bayelsa-discovers-28000-ghost-workers.html (Accessed on June 30, 2019).

Premium Times. 2016. "CBN recruitment scandal: Job titles for Buhari, Ministers' relatives released." http://www.premiumtimesng.com/news/top-news/201055-cbn-recruitment-scandal-job-titles-buhari-ministers-relatives-released.html. March 30.

Public Service Commission. 2014a. *Towards a Conceptual Framework for a Developmental State in South Africa*. Pretoria: Public Service Commission.

Public Service Commission. 2014b. "The Nature, Characteristics and Leadership of the Public Service of Malaysia." Report of a Study Visit. http://www.psc.gov.za/conferences/dev-state-conference/Dev%20State%20Papers/Report%20of%20the%20study%20tour%20to%20Malaysia.pdf. (Accessed on September 23, 2018).

Punch. 2018a. "Ibori ensured Okwa emerged Governor from UK Prison – Secondus". March 11. https://punchng.com/ibori-ensured-okowa-emerged-gov-from-uk-prison-secondus/ (Accessed on April 3, 2019).

Punch. 2018b. "Presidential Primary: Dollar Rain as Saraki, Atiku, Tambuwal Divide PDP Leaders". *The Punch,* October 7. https://punchng.com/dollar-rain-as-saraki-atiku-tambuwal-divide-pdp-leaders/ (Accessed on January 12, 2019).

Punch. 2018c. "80 per cent of Niger Delta Revenues Diverted to Private Bank Accounts–EFCC." September 15. https://punchng.com/80-per-cent-of-ndelta-revenues-diverted-to-private-bank-accounts-efcc/ (Accessed on September 15, 2019).

Punch. 2016. "Kaduna Removes over 13,000 Workers from Payroll". June 25. https://punchng.com/kaduna-removes-13000-workers-payroll/ (Accessed on September 28, 2018).

Sahara Reporters. 2016a. "45 Percent of Nigerian Graduates Unemployed: Survey." January 25. http://saharareporters.com/2016/01/25/45-percent-nigerian-graduates-unemployed-survey (Accessed on June 20, 2018).

Sahara Reporters. 2016b. "Revealed : Positions Allocated to Privileged Relatives of President Buhari's Top Officials and Associates in Illegal CBN Employment". March 29. http://saharareporters.com/2016/03/29/revealed-positions-allocated-privileged-relatives-president-buhari%E2%80%99s-top-officials-and (Accessed on March 30, 2019).

Samura, Brima K. 2009. "The Negative Effects of Corruption on Developing Nations." https://www.carl-sl.org/pres/the-negative-effects-of-corruption-on-developing-nations-a-perspective-on-sierra-leones-effort-to/ (Accessed on June 12, 2018).

Sen, Amartya. 1990. *Development as Freedom*. Oxford: Oxford University Press

Soludo, Chukwuma C. 2015. "President Jonathan Missed the Point on the Missing N30 Trillion". *Sahara Reporters*, February 24. http://saharareporters.com/2015/02/24/president-jonathan-missed-point-missing-n30-trillion-chukwuma-charles-soludo. (Accessed on June 21, 2017).

Southall, Roger. 2013. *Liberation movements in Power: Party and State in Southern Africa*. UK: James Currey.

The Cable. 2018. "Gulak: I Was Offered $2 Million To Manipulate Imo Guber Primary." November 10. https://www.thecable.ng/gulak-i-was-offered-2-million-to-manipulate-imo-gov-primaries. (Accessed on December 10, 2018).

The Economist. 2016. "Business in Africa: 1.2 Billion Opportunities." https://www.economist.com/special-report/2016/04/14/12-billion-opportunities (Accessed on November 10, 2019).

The Guardian. 2018. "Editorial: This Crisis-Prone National Assembly!" August 24. http://guardian.ng/opinion/this-crisis-prone-national-assembly/amp/? (Accessed on January 10, 2019).

The Sun. 2017. "Abandoned N12trn Projects". November 12. http://sunnewsonline.com/abandoned-n12trn-projects/ (Accessed on August 24, 2018).

UNESCO. 2015. "Education for All 2000 – 2015: No Countries in Sub-Saharan Africa Reached Global Education Goals." http://en.unesco.org/gem-report/sites/gem-report/files/SSA_PR_en.pdf. (Accessed on December 4, 2017).

United Nations. 2015. *The Millennium Development Goals Report, 2015*. New York: United Nations.

United Nations. 1997. "If Information and Knowledge are Central to Democracy, They are Conditions For Development, Says Secretary-General". June 23. https://www.un.org/press/en/1997/19970623.sgsm6268.html. (Accessed on July 10, 2018).

United Nations Children's Fund. 2015. "Maternal mortality declined by 38 per cent between 2000 and 2017". https://data.unicef.org/topic/maternal-health/maternal-mortality/ (Accessed on June 28, 2018).

United Nations Conference on Trade and Development. 2015. *World Investment Report 2015: Reforming International Investment Governance*. Geneva: UNCTAD.

United Nations Conference on Trade and Development. 2009. *The State and Development Governance: The Least Developed Countries Report*. New York and Geneva: UNCTAD.

United Nations Development Programme. 2013. *World Development Report*. New York: UNDP.

United Nations Department of Economic Affairs. 1951. *Measures for The Economic Development of Under-Developed Countries*. Report / By A Group of Experts Appointed By The Secretary-General Of The United Nations. E/1986 ST/ECA/10. May. New York: UN.

United Nations Economic Commission for Africa. 2016. *Measuring Corruption in Africa: the International Dimension Matters*. Addis Ababa: ECA.

United Nations Economic Commission for Africa. 2011. "Economic Report on Africa 2011: Governing Development in Africa – The Role of The State in Economic Transformation". https://www.uneca.org/publications/economic-report-africa-2011. (Accessed on May 12, 2018).

Usman, Solomon A. 2015. "Unemployment and poverty as sources and consequence of insecurity in Nigeria: The Boko Haram Insurgency Revisited." *African Journal of Political Science and International Relations*. 9 (3): 90 – 99.

Utomi, Pat. 2016a. "The Class of '66 and How They Destroy Nigeria". December 25. https://www.thetrentonline.com/pat-utomi-class-66-nigeria/. (Accessed on August 30, 2018).

Utomi, Pat. 2016b. "The Class of '66 has held Nigeria Captive for 50 Years." https://abujareporters.com.ng/the-class-of-66-has-held-nigeria-captive-for-50-years-pat-utomi/. (Accessed on September 19, 2019).

Vanguard. 2019. "Oshiomhole Lacks the Temperament Required to Lead a Political Party – Oyegun." *Vanguard*. June 2. https://www.vanguardngr.com/2019/06/oshiomhole-lacks-the-temperament-required-to-lead-a-political-party-oyegun-fires-back/ (Accessed on June 2, 2019).

Vanguard. 2018. "PIB: Nigeria Loses N3trn Annually over Non-passage." July 4. https://www.vanguardngr.com/2018/07/pib-nigeria-loses-n3trn-annually-over-non-passage/ (Accessed on July 28, 2018).

Weiss, Linda. 2010. "Transformative Capacity and the Developmental States: Lessons for South Africa." Public Lecture presented at the Policy Analysis Unit/Centre for Africa's Social Progress, Human Sciences Research Council, February 18, Pretoria, South Africa.

White, Gordon. 1998. "Constructing a Democratic Developmental State." In. Mark Robinson and Gordon White, ed. *The Democratic Developmental State: Political and Institutional Design*. Oxford: Oxford University Press.

World Bank. 2018a. "World Development Indicators." https://data.worldbank.org/indicator/NY.GDP.PCAP.PP.KD?locations=NG. (Accessed on August 20, 2018).

World Bank. 2018b. *World Development Report: Learning to Realize Education's Promise*. Washington DC: The World Bank Group.

World Bank.2018c. "Poverty and Equity Data Portal." http://povertydata.worldbank.org/poverty/country/NGA. (Accessed on August 22, 2019).

World Bank. 2018d. "World Development Indicators." .https://data.worldbank.org/indicator/SH.XPD.CHEX.GD.ZS) (August 22, 2019).

World Bank. 2017a. "World Development Indicators: Poverty Rates at International Poverty Lines." http://wdi.worldbank.org/table/1.2. (Accessed on August 21, 2018).

World Bank. 2017b. "Public trust in Politicians." https://tcdata360.worldbank.org/indicators/h45ea0a18?country=BR A&indicator=665&countries=NGA&viz=line_chart&years=2007,2 017. (Accessed on January 6, 2018).

World Bank. 2016a. *Poverty and Shared Prosperity 2016: Taking on Inequality.* Washington DC: The World Bank Group.

World Bank. 2016b. "World Development Indicators." March 29. http://documents.worldbank.org/curated/en/805371467990952829/ World-development-indicators-2016 (Accessed on March 30, 2016).

World Economic Forum. 2018. "Efficiency of government spending." Executive Opinion Survey. http://reports.weforum.org/pdf/gci-2017-2018-scorecard/WEF_GCI_2017_2018_Scorecard_EOSQ043.pdf. (Accessed on July 1, 2019).

World Economic Forum. 2017. *World Economic Forum Global Competitiveness, 2017–2018.*Geneva: World Economic Forum. http://www3.weforum.org/docs/GCR2017-2018/05FullReport/TheGlobalCompetitivenessReport2017%E2%8 0%932018.pdf. (Accessed on August 30, 2019).

World Health Organization (WHO). 2018. *World Health Statistics 2018: Monitoring Health for SDGs, Sustainable Development Goals.* Geneva: World Health Organization.

Index

Nigeria: Democracy without Development. How to fix it

Nigeria: Democracy without Development. How to fix it

Nigeria: Democracy without Development. How to fix it

Appendix 1

KANO EMIRATE COUNC

COUNCIL SECRETARIAT

OFFICE ADDRESS:
Opposite Emir's Palace,
Kano City,
Nigeria.

P.M.B. 3002, KANO,

Ref: KEC/STM/14A/VOL.1/2017/1.8

Date: 22ⁿᵈ December, 2017

The Chairman
Federal Civil Service Commission,
Abjan Street
Wuse Zone 3/ Garki
Abuja.

APPLICATION FOR EMPLOYMENT

I am directed to refer the under mentioned applicants to your good office. They have sought our father's assistance of the Council in their request to your consideration. They are:

1. Noshin Ngozi Morenike 05080782947
2. Aitechi Agabza James 08033603555
3. Likam Victoria Ihetuma 080813459194
4. Ugwuagu Omere Yardon – 07934809809
5. Yuchima Ekhibama Dikki – 0706743U196

We hope their applications will be accorded with a special attention base on their eligibility paper.

Accept our best regards.

(Awaisu Abdu Idrissi)
H. E. O. (Admin.)
For: Secretary, Kano Emirate Council

About the Author

Dr Omano Edigheji is a scholar and development expert. He holds a PhD in Political Science, with a specialisation in the political economy of development, from the Norwegian University of Science and Technology (Trondheim, Norway).

Dr Edigheji has over twenty years' experience in government, the academia, not-for-profit development foundations and civil society.

He founded and was CEO of Zeezi Oasis Leadership Inspiration Ltd, a consulting and leadership development firm based in Abuja. Dr Edigheji was also the Lead Consultant of the African Higher Education Programme, TrustAfrica. He was also Chief Technical Adviser, Public Service Reform at the Public Service Commission of South Africa. In this capacity, he led the reforms process to build a professional, career and capable public service in South Africa. Prior to that, Dr Edigheji was Research Director at the Human Sciences Research Council, South Africa and headed the Council's research and policy programme on State and Economic Development. Also, he was Research Manager at the Johannesburg based policy think-tank, Centre for Policy Studies.

Dr Edigheji has served as consultant to the New Partnership for Africa's Development (NEPAD) Agency, the United Nations Economic Commission for Africa (UNECA), the United Nations Institute for Economic Development and Planning (IDEP), the

German Agency for International Cooperation (GIZ), African Development Bank (AfDB), and International Institute for Democracy and Electoral Assistance (International IDEA).

Dr Edigheji has convened and facilitated a number of multi-stakeholder forums on issues of human rights, public sector reform, industrial development, economic reform and higher education transformation. He was the Director of the first-ever continental summit on African Higher Education that took place in Dakar, Senegal in March 2015.

Dr Edigheji has published extensively, including three books, '*The Future and Relevance of Nigerian Universities and other Tertiary Institutions*' (co-editor, September 2016); '*Constructing a Democratic Developmental State in South Africa: Potentials and Challenges* (editor, HSRC Press, 2010); and *Governance in the New South Africa: The Challenges of Globalization* (co-editor, University of Cape Town Press, 2003).

Dr Edigheji has lectured at the University of Witwatersrand, Johannesburg and the Nelson Mandela Metropolitan University, Port Elizabeth, both in South Africa.

In the course of completing this book, the Governor of Kaduna State, Mallam Nasir Ahmad El-Rufai appointed him as his Special Adviser, Research and Documentation.

About the Author

Nigeria: Democracy without Development. How to fix it

Printed in Great Britain
by Amazon